Deep Learning for Geospatial Intelligence

Techniques, Applications, and Insights

[†] Dr. Babasaheb Ambedkar Technological University, Lonere, India

Deep Learning for Geospatial Intelligence

Dr. Geetanjali Sameer Mahamunkar

30th April 2025

To my husband and my kids

Dr. Geetanjali Sameer Mahamunkar

"The goal is to turn data into information, and information into insight."

CARLY FIORINA

Preface

In recent years, we have witnessed a remarkable convergence: the explosive growth of geospatial data and the rapid advancement of deep learning techniques. From high-resolution satellite imagery and LiDAR scans to drone footage and crowdsourced maps, our ability to observe the Earth has evolved beyond what was once imaginable. But the true power of this data lies not just in its collection, but in its intelligent interpretation.

This book was born out of a desire to bridge two dynamic fields—Remote Sensing and Artificial Intelligence—and to explore how deep learning can unlock new insights from complex geospatial data.

The book is structured in a way that gradually introduces the reader to foundational knowledge, implementation skills, and applied case studies before moving into future trends and research directions. Here's how the content flows:

- **Part I: Theoretical Foundations** – Introduces the basics of geospatial data, remote sensing, and deep learning architectures.
- **Part II: Methodologies and Tools** – Equips students with the platforms and frameworks (like QGIS, GEE, TensorFlow) used in real-world projects.
- **Part III: Applications and Case Studies** – Demonstrates how deep learning is applied in real-world geospatial challenges such as mangrove mapping, LULC classification, landslide prediction, and black spot detection.
- **Part IV: Emerging Frontiers and Vision** – Discusses emerging topics like Geospatial AI for sustainability, federated learning, and student research opportunities.

This structured approach ensures that readers move from conceptual understanding to hands-on practice and are then inspired to contribute to cutting-edge geospatial research. I hope that readers will find not only technical knowledge within these pages, but also motivation to use these tools in service of sustainable, intelligent decision-making.

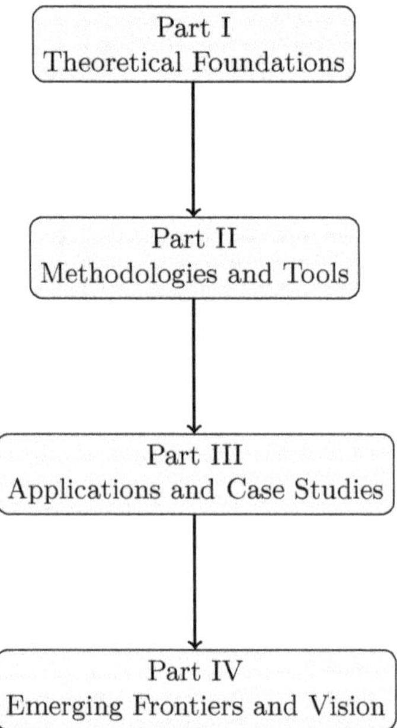

Figure 1: Flow of Content Across Book Parts

Dr. Geetanjali Sameer Mahamunkar

Acknowledgement

This book would not have been possible without the support, encouragement, and insight of many people who accompanied me on this academic journey.

First, I would like to express my deepest gratitude to my mentors and colleagues at Dr. Babasaheb Ambedkar Technological University. Your guidance helped shape the foundation of this work and provided invaluable academic direction.

To my research collaborators and students, your enthusiasm, questions, and curiosity fueled much of the content in this book. Our discussions—ranging from neural network optimization to preprocessing satellite images—greatly enriched my understanding and sharpened the focus of each chapter.

To the open-source geospatial community, your commitment to transparency, reproducibility, and innovation provided both the tools and the inspiration to make this book accessible to a wider audience. Platforms like QGIS, Google Earth Engine, and GitHub demonstrate the power of shared knowledge.

To my family—especially my husband and children—thank you for your unwavering patience and love. Your belief in me and your understanding during late nights of writing and reviewing never went unnoticed.

Lastly, I dedicate this work to the next generation of geospatial thinkers and builders. May this book serve as a stepping stone for your ideas, research, and vision to build a better, data-informed world.

Dr. Geetanjali Sameer Mahamunkar

Contents

IV Emerging Frontiers and Vision   101

11 Geospatial AI for Climate Action and Sustainability   103

12 Future Directions and Student Research Opportunities   111

Part I

Theoretical Foundations

Chapter 1

Geospatial Data and Remote Sensing – A Primer

Learning Objectives

At the end of this chapter, you should be able to:

- Define geospatial data and remote sensing.
- Distinguish between vector and raster data.
- Describe basic remote sensing principles.
- Classify sensors and their key parameters.
- Understand the preprocessing steps for remote sensing data.
- Identify common geospatial data formats and their uses.

1.1   Introduction

In an era characterized by rapid environmental change, urbanization, and the imperative for sustainable development, geospatial data and remote sensing technologies have become critical tools for the systematic observation, analysis, and management of Earth's resources. This chapter provides a comprehensive overview of geospatial science, detailing its core principles, the historical evolution of remote sensing, and the integration of these domains for the interpretation of complex Earth systems. The significance of these technologies in facilitating data-driven decision-making across sectors such as environmental management, urban planning, agriculture, and disaster mitigation is also emphasized. As the capacity to capture, process, and interpret geospatial information has grown, its application has become indispensable in addressing contemporary global challenges.

This chapter serves as a foundation for the subsequent integration of geospatial science with deep learning methodologies, which will be explored in later chapters.

1.2   What is Geospatial Data?

Geospatial data, also known as spatial data, refers to information linked to specific geographic locations. This data can be expressed in various forms, including coordinates (latitude and longitude), addresses, and place names. Geospatial data encompasses two primary types: vector and raster data.

1.2.1   Vector Data

Vector data represents discrete geographic features such as points, lines, and polygons. Points could denote locations like city centers, while lines represent features such as roads or rivers, and polygons represent areas like administrative boundaries. Common formats for vector data include Shapefile and GeoJSON.

1.2.2   Raster Data

Raster data, on the other hand, is composed of grid-based pixels. Each pixel carries a value corresponding to a specific attribute such as land surface temperature, elevation, or vegetation index. Raster data is commonly used in remote sensing applications, where it allows the analysis of continuous phenomena like temperature or vegetation distribution.

Table 1.1: Comparison of Vector and Raster Data Characteristics

Feature	Vector Data	Raster Data
Structure	Points, lines, polygons	Grid of pixels
Storage Format	Shapefile, GeoJSON, KML	TIFF, JPEG, HDF
Common Uses	Infrastructure mapping	Satellite imagery, terrain models
Spatial Precision	High	Depends on pixel resolution

1.3   Fundamentals of Remote Sensing

Remote sensing involves the acquisition of data about Earth's surface without direct contact. This process typically utilizes satellite or airborne sensors and can be classified into two primary categories: passive and active remote sensing.

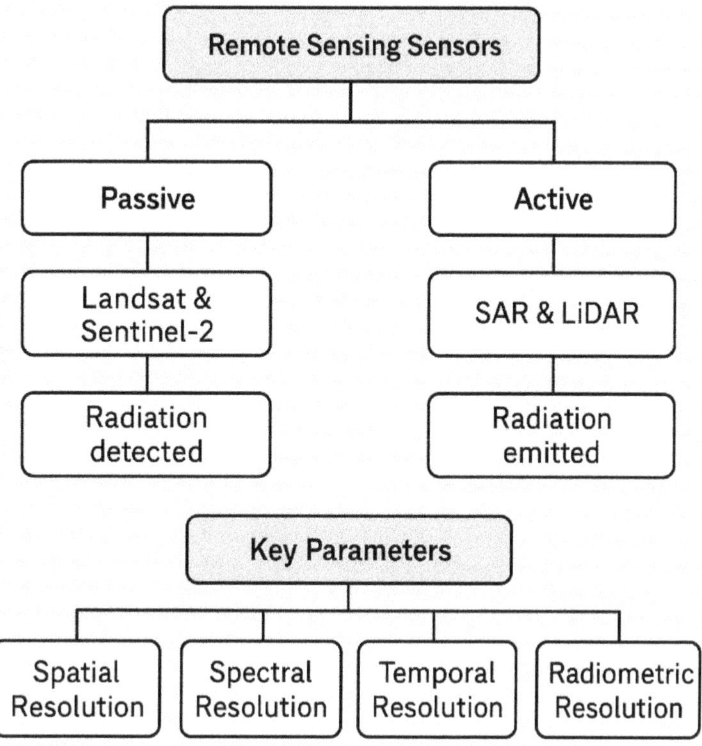

Figure 1.1: Classification of sensors and their key parameters.

1.3.1 Passive Remote Sensing

Passive remote sensing detects natural energy, primarily solar radiation reflected by the Earth. Instruments such as Landsat and Sentinel-2 are examples of passive sensors that capture this reflected energy.

1.3.2 Active Remote Sensing

Active remote sensing systems emit energy and measure the return signal. Synthetic Aperture Radar (SAR) and LiDAR are prominent examples of active sensors that provide valuable data irrespective of solar illumination.

Key components of remote sensing include platforms (e.g., satellites, aircraft, UAVs), sensors (which measure electromagnetic radiation), and various types of resolution (spatial, spectral, temporal, and radiometric). These resolutions are fundamental in selecting appropriate datasets for specific applications, especially those utilizing deep learning methods.

1.4   Evolution of Remote Sensing Technologies

Remote sensing technologies have evolved significantly over the past century, from early aerial photography to modern high-resolution, multispectral, and real-time satellite systems. Key milestones in the development of remote sensing include:

- **1972**: Launch of Landsat 1 by NASA.
- **1980s–1990s**: Commercial Earth observation technologies emerged, with satellites like SPOT and IKONOS.
- **2000s**: Open-access satellite data became widely available, with platforms like MODIS and Sentinel.
- **2010s onward**: The integration of CubeSats, cloud computing, and real-time analytics has enhanced remote sensing capabilities.

These advancements have democratized data access, increased the temporal and spatial frequency of Earth observations, and improved the usability of geospatial data in decision-making processes.

1.5   Types of Satellite Data and Their Applications

Satellite data can be categorized into several types based on the sensors' capabilities, each suited for different applications. These include multispectral, hyperspectral, thermal infrared, and radar (SAR) data.

1.5.1   Multispectral Data

Multispectral data refers to reflectance measurements across multiple discrete spectral bands. Platforms such as Landsat and Sentinel-2 provide multispectral data, which is widely used in applications like vegetation analysis and land cover classification.

1.5.2   Hyperspectral Data

Hyperspectral data captures data in hundreds of contiguous spectral bands, providing finer discrimination of material properties. This data is useful for applications such as mineral identification and vegetation species classification.

1.5.3   Thermal Infrared Data

Thermal infrared data measures heat emitted from objects. It is useful for monitoring urban heat islands, detecting fire and geothermal activity, and conducting industrial thermal audits.

1.5.4 Radar and Microwave Data (SAR)

Synthetic Aperture Radar (SAR) data is valuable for all-weather, day-and-night monitoring. It is commonly used in flood mapping, surface deformation studies, and monitoring glaciers and forests.

1.6 Data Acquisition and Preprocessing

Efficient use of remote sensing data requires systematic preprocessing. Key preprocessing steps include:

- **Radiometric Correction**: Rectifying distortions caused by the sensor or atmospheric conditions.
- **Geometric Correction**: Ensuring spatial alignment with real-world coordinates.
- **Cloud Masking**: Identifying and excluding cloud-covered areas.
- **Image Enhancement**: Improving image quality through techniques like contrast stretching and edge enhancement.
- **Data Fusion**: Combining multiple datasets to improve spatial or temporal resolution.

Preprocessing is critical for deep learning applications, where annotated datasets and normalization techniques are essential for effective model training.

1.7 Role of GIS in Remote Sensing

Geographic Information Systems (GIS) provide the analytical framework for integrating remote sensing data with other spatial datasets. GIS allows for the overlay of multiple spatial layers, terrain modeling, proximity analysis, and predictive modeling. By merging remote sensing data with demographic, ecological, and infrastructure information, GIS enhances decision-making capabilities and supports advanced spatial analysis.

1.8 Emerging Trends in Geospatial Technology

Recent developments in geospatial technology are being driven by advancements in cloud-based analytics, machine learning, smart sensors, and digital twin Earth models. Emerging trends include:

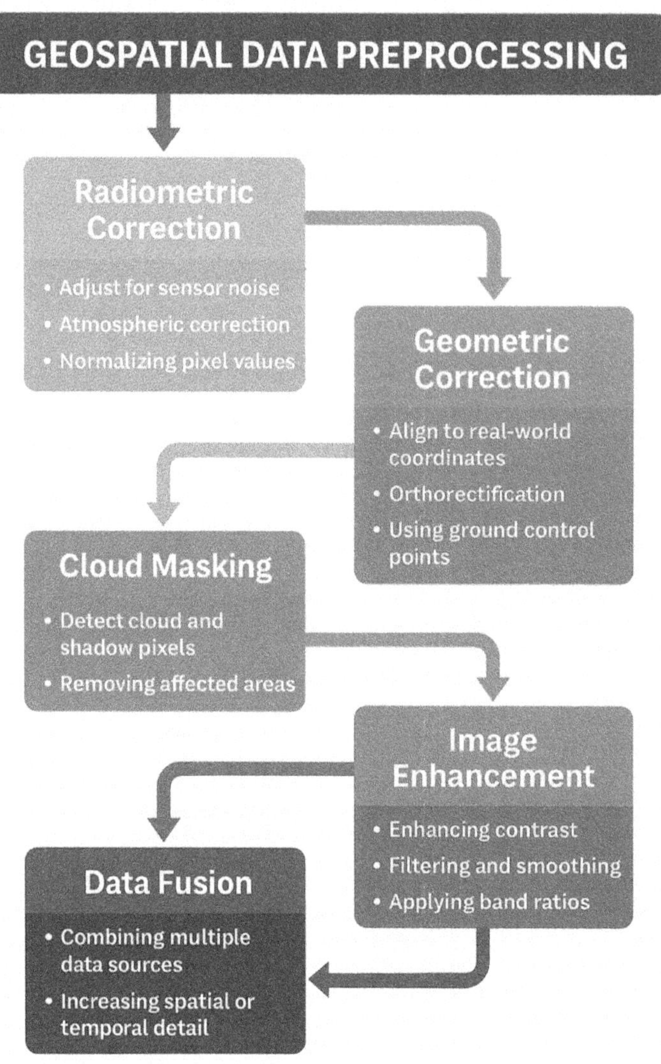

Figure 1.2: Geospatial Data Preprocessing Workflow

- **Cloud-Based Analytics**: Platforms like Google Earth Engine facilitate large-scale geospatial analysis.
- **Machine Learning and AI**: These techniques automate classification, object detection, and change analysis.
- **Smart Sensors and IoT**: Real-time environmental monitoring is increasingly integrated into geospatial frameworks.
- **Digital Twin Earth Models**: Virtual representations of Earth systems are used for simulation and planning.

These trends are reshaping the future of geospatial technology, making it more accessible, scalable, and capable of addressing complex global challenges.

1.9 Challenges in Working with Geospatial Data

Despite its potential, working with geospatial data presents several challenges, including:

- **Data Volume**: Handling large volumes of geospatial data, especially in real-time applications.
- **Heterogeneity**: Harmonizing data from diverse sensors and sources.
- **Artifacts**: Managing noise introduced by atmospheric conditions.
- **Licensing**: Navigating the complexities of data licensing, both commercial and open.
- **Technical Skills**: The need for proficiency in programming, GIS, and remote sensing technologies.

1.10 Summary and Future Directions

This chapter provided a comprehensive overview of geospatial data and remote sensing, highlighting their fundamental principles, evolution, and applications. As geospatial technologies continue to advance, the integration of deep learning and AI with remote sensing data will enable more sophisticated analysis and decision-making, addressing global challenges with unprecedented precision. Future directions include the continued development of real-time Earth observation systems, enhanced predictive modeling, and the widespread adoption of cloud-based geospatial analytics.

The following chapters will explore these technologies in greater detail, focusing on their role in sustainable development and resource management.

Exercise Questions

(1) Differentiate between active and passive remote sensing with examples.

(2) What are the key steps in preprocessing satellite imagery?

(3) Compare vector and raster data models based on structure, precision, and use-cases.

(4) Explain the significance of radiometric and geometric corrections in image preprocessing.

(5) Describe any two types of sensors and their applications.

Notes and Suggestions

- Remote sensing is a rapidly evolving field—staying updated with satellite missions (like Sentinel, Landsat) is recommended.
- Practice image preprocessing using tools like QGIS, SNAP, or ERDAS Imagine.
- Understanding the basic physics behind sensors enhances interpretation skills.

Chapter 2

Foundations of Deep Learning for Geospatial Applications

Learning Objectives

At the end of this chapter, you should be able to:

- Understand the fundamentals of deep learning
- Identify key deep learning architectures
- Familiarize themselves with common deep learning workflows
- Recognize specialized deep learning frameworks and libraries
- Evaluate models using common metrics
- Discuss challenges and considerations

2.1   Introduction

Deep learning, a subset of artificial intelligence (AI), has revolutionized many fields by enabling machines to learn complex patterns directly from data. Geospatial data, which encompasses spatial information about Earth's surface (like satellite images, remote sensing data, or GIS datasets), can be massive, complex, and multidimensional. Deep learning techniques have emerged as a powerful tool to process and analyze these datasets, enabling more accurate decision-making in various applications such as environmental monitoring, urban planning, and disaster management.

Geospatial data comes from various sources such as satellite imagery, sensor networks, and geographic information systems (GIS). The sheer volume and complexity of this data present significant challenges for traditional analytical methods, making deep learning a promising solution. Deep learning's ability to automatically extract features, capture complex relationships, and scale to large datasets makes it ideal for applications in geospatial intelligence, where high-dimensional data is common.

2.2 Why Deep Learning for Geospatial Intelligence?

2.2.1 Volume and Variety

Geospatial datasets are often large and complex, making them difficult to handle using traditional machine learning methods. For example, satellite data from sources like Sentinel or Landsat consists of multiple spectral bands, capturing different features of Earth's surface over time and space. These datasets can contain millions of data points, making them "high-dimensional."

Traditional machine learning algorithms often require substantial preprocessing to extract meaningful features from raw data, such as satellite images. However, the variety in the data (e.g., various geographic features, temporal patterns, and sensor types) makes it difficult to engineer features manually without losing critical information. This is where deep learning comes in.

Deep learning models, such as convolutional neural networks (CNNs), are well-suited for handling high-dimensional data because they can work directly with raw data and automatically learn the most important features. These models can learn hierarchical representations of data, which means they can automatically extract features from lower-level (raw) data, such as edges in an image, and build up to more complex patterns, such as vegetation or urban structures.

2.2.2 Complex Non-linear Patterns

Many geospatial phenomena, such as urban sprawl, land degradation, or climate change impacts, follow non-linear patterns that are difficult to model using traditional regression techniques. Traditional models often assume linear relationships between input and output variables, but geospatial data is inherently complex and does not always fit into simple linear patterns. For instance, the relationship between the urban heat island effect and land cover types may be complex and non-linear, requiring sophisticated techniques to model effectively.

Deep learning models, particularly neural networks with multiple layers (hence, the term "deep" learning), are designed to capture these complex, non-linear relationships. Each layer in a deep neural network performs transformations on the data, learning increasingly abstract representations at each stage. These layers help the model capture intricate, non-linear patterns that traditional models might miss, which is especially important for geospatial data that exhibits spatial and temporal non-linearity.

2.2.3 Automation of Feature Engineering

In traditional machine learning, feature engineering—the process of manually selecting and designing features from raw data—is essential for improving model performance. This often requires domain expertise and can be time-consuming. For example, in satellite imagery, experts may use specific indices, such as the Normalized Difference Vegetation Index (NDVI), to assess vegetation health, or they may rely on manually designed textures or statistical measures of the image to classify land cover types.

However, deep learning models can automate the feature extraction process. Models like CNNs do not require manually crafted features. Instead, they learn the most relevant features directly from the raw data during training. By applying layers of convolution and pooling operations, CNNs can extract hierarchical patterns and features, such as edges, textures, or shapes, automatically from satellite images.

This automated approach reduces the need for expert knowledge and allows deep learning models to scale better across various datasets and tasks. In addition, it helps reduce human biases and errors that may arise from manual feature selection.

2.2.4 Transfer Learning

One of the challenges in applying deep learning to geospatial data is the limited availability of labeled data. Training deep neural networks typically requires large, labeled datasets, which can be expensive and time-consuming to gather, especially for specialized geospatial tasks. Collecting large amounts of labeled data for a task such as land cover classification or flood detection may not always be feasible.

Transfer learning is a technique that allows models to leverage knowledge learned from one task and apply it to another related task. The approach involves taking a pre-trained model (usually trained on large, general datasets such as ImageNet) and fine-tuning it on a smaller, task-specific dataset. By using a pre-trained model, the network can learn general patterns from the large dataset and then adapt these patterns to solve the specialized task with fewer labeled examples.

For instance, a pre-trained model that has learned to detect objects in general images (like vehicles, animals, or buildings) can be fine-tuned on satellite images to detect specific geospatial features such as roads or forests. This significantly reduces the data requirements for training deep learning models for geospatial tasks.

2.3   Neural Networks: A Primer

2.3.1   Basic Architecture

Neural networks consist of several key components that work together to process and learn from data:

- **Input Layer:** The input layer is where data enters the neural network. In geospatial applications, this could be a satellite image, a time-series of sensor readings, or a vector of GIS data. The data is passed from the input layer to the subsequent hidden layers for processing.
- **Hidden Layers:** Hidden layers are the core components of a neural network, performing computations on the input data. Each hidden layer consists of neurons, which receive weighted inputs, apply a transformation (using an activation function), and pass the results to the next layer. In deep neural networks, there are multiple hidden layers that extract increasingly abstract features from the raw data.
- **Output Layer:** The output layer produces the final prediction of the model. For example, in a classification task, the output layer might produce a probability distribution over possible classes (e.g., land cover types). In a regression task, the output might be a continuous value (e.g., the amount of rainfall).

Each layer in the network has its own parameters (weights and biases) that are learned during training. The layers work together to progressively transform the input data into meaningful predictions.

2.3.2   Activation Functions

Activation functions are a critical component of neural networks as they introduce non-linearity to the model. Without activation functions, a neural network would only be able to model linear relationships, limiting its ability to capture complex patterns.

Common activation functions include:

- **Sigmoid:** The sigmoid function maps input values to a range between 0 and 1. It is often used for binary classification tasks, such as detecting the presence or absence of a particular feature in geospatial data.

- **Tanh:** The tanh function maps input values between -1 and 1, helping to center the data around zero. This can be beneficial in situations where the data has both positive and negative values.
- **ReLU (Rectified Linear Unit):** The ReLU function outputs zero for negative inputs and the input itself for positive values. It is the most commonly used activation function because it is computationally efficient and reduces the likelihood of vanishing gradients during training.
- **Leaky ReLU & ELU:** These are variations of ReLU that aim to fix the "dying ReLU" problem, where neurons become inactive and stop learning. Leaky ReLU allows a small, non-zero gradient for negative inputs, while ELU introduces an exponential term to handle negative inputs more effectively.

2.3.3 Loss Functions

Loss functions are used to measure how well a model's predictions match the actual data. The goal of training a neural network is to minimize the loss function, thereby improving the model's accuracy.

Common loss functions include:

- **Binary Cross-Entropy:** Used for binary classification tasks. This loss function compares the predicted probability of the two classes to the true class labels.
- **Categorical Cross-Entropy:** Used for multi-class classification tasks, such as classifying different land cover types. This loss function measures the difference between the predicted class probabilities and the actual class labels.
- **MSE (Mean Squared Error):** Used for regression tasks, such as predicting continuous variables like temperature or vegetation height. MSE calculates the average of the squared differences between predicted and actual values.
- **MAE (Mean Absolute Error):** Similar to MSE, but it measures the absolute differences between predicted and actual values. MAE is less sensitive to outliers than MSE.

2.3.4 Optimization Algorithms

Optimization algorithms are used to adjust the weights and biases in a neural network to minimize the loss function. These algorithms are critical for improving model performance.

Common optimization algorithms include:

- **SGD (Stochastic Gradient Descent):** The most basic optimization algorithm, which updates the model's weights based on a random sample of the data. This process helps the model converge to a solution by gradually reducing the error.

- **Momentum:** Momentum builds upon SGD by considering the past gradients when updating the model's weights, helping to smooth the updates and accelerate convergence.
- **Adam:** Adam combines the advantages of both SGD and Momentum. It adjusts the learning rate for each parameter and adapts the learning rate during training, leading to more efficient optimization.

2.4 Comparison of Deep Learning Architectures for Geospatial Data

Table 2.1: Comparison of Common Deep Learning Architectures for Geospatial Applications

Model	Structure	Best For	Geospatial Use Case
MLP	Fully connected layers	Tabular data	Soil classification
CNN	Convolution + pooling	Image data	Land cover mapping
RNN	Recurrent units (LSTM/GRU)	Temporal data	Crop phenology modeling

2.5 Multilayer Perceptrons (MLPs)

Multilayer Perceptrons (MLPs) are one of the foundational architectures in deep learning. They are composed of multiple layers of neurons, where each neuron in one layer is connected to every neuron in the next layer. This type of network is known as a fully connected network.

2.5.1 Structure of MLP

- **Input Layer**: Takes in the input features, such as spatial attributes like elevation, land use type, or vegetation index.
- **Hidden Layers**: One or more intermediate layers where the actual computation takes place. Each neuron applies a weighted sum followed by an activation function (like ReLU or sigmoid).
- **Output Layer**: Produces the final prediction—such as a class label or continuous value.

2.5.2 Working Principle

Each neuron in a hidden layer performs the following steps:

(1) Takes the weighted sum of inputs from the previous layer.

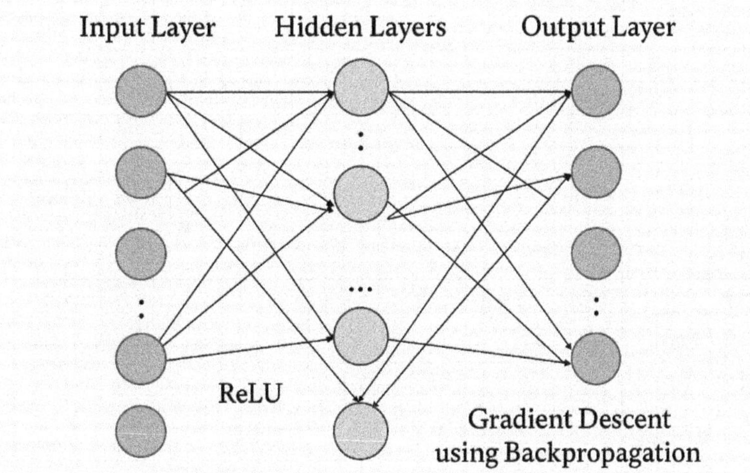

Figure 2.1: MLP Architecture

(2) Adds a bias term.

(3) Passes the result through a non-linear activation function.

This process enables the network to learn non-linear relationships between input features and the output.

2.5.3 Applications in Geospatial Domain

- **Soil Classification**: Predict soil type from attributes like pH, organic matter content, and texture.
- **Climate Zoning**: Classify regions based on temperature, precipitation, and elevation data.
- **Yield Prediction**: Estimate crop yield using numerical features from remote sensing and field data.

2.5.4 Advantages and Limitations

Advantages:

- Simple to implement and interpret.
- Works well on small to medium-sized tabular datasets.

Limitations:

- Struggles with spatial or sequential data without modification.
- Prone to overfitting if the number of layers or neurons is too high.

2.6 Convolutional Neural Networks (CNNs) and Geospatial Imagery

Convolutional Neural Networks (CNNs) are specialized neural networks designed for processing data with a grid-like topology, such as images. Their design allows them to effectively learn spatial hierarchies and extract patterns from image data.

2.6.1 Structure of CNN

- **Input Layer**: Receives image data—e.g., multispectral satellite imagery.
- **Convolutional Layers**: Apply learnable filters to detect features like edges, textures, and shapes.
- **Activation Function**: Typically uses ReLU to introduce non-linearity.
- **Pooling Layers**: Reduce dimensionality by summarizing features (e.g., max pooling).
- **Fully Connected Layers**: Toward the end, flatten feature maps to connect to output neurons.
- **Output Layer**: Produces a final prediction—e.g., classifying the land cover type.

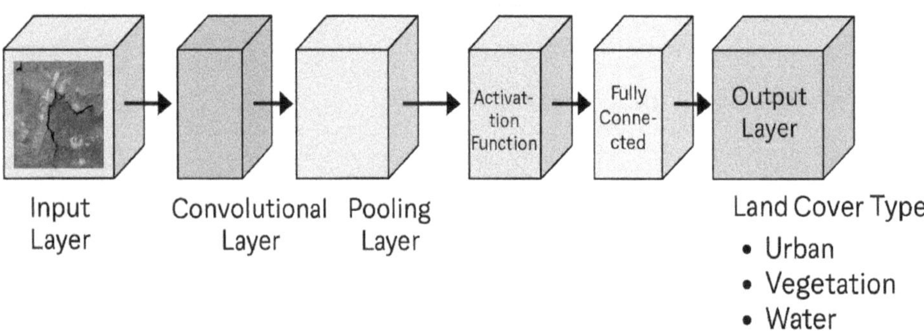

Figure 2.2: CNN for Classifying Landcover Type

2.6.2 Working Principle

The CNN works by:

(1) Extracting spatial features using convolution operations.
(2) Applying non-linearity through activation functions.
(3) Downsampling using pooling to focus on the most prominent features.
(4) Using fully connected layers to classify based on learned features.

This architecture enables CNNs to detect spatially invariant features, making them powerful for image-based geospatial tasks.

2.6.3 Applications in Geospatial Domain

- **Land Use and Land Cover Classification**: Categorizing land areas based on satellite imagery.
- **Urban Feature Detection**: Identifying roads, buildings, and other infrastructure.
- **Water Body and Forest Segmentation**: Delineating water or vegetation from multispectral data.
- **Disaster Impact Mapping**: Detecting changes post-flood or earthquake using before-after image pairs.

2.6.4 Popular CNN Architectures

- **VGGNet**: Known for its simplicity and uniform architecture, good for image classification.
- **ResNet**: Introduces residual connections to train very deep networks effectively.
- **U-Net**: Specially designed for semantic segmentation, widely used in geospatial imagery.

2.6.5 Advantages and Limitations

Advantages:

- Automatically learns spatial features from images.
- Effective for high-resolution image analysis and segmentation.

Limitations:

- Requires large datasets and high computational resources.
- Sensitive to variations in scale and resolution if not handled properly.

2.7 Recurrent Neural Networks (RNNs) for Temporal Geospatial Data

Recurrent Neural Networks (RNNs) are designed to handle sequential data, making them highly suitable for tasks involving temporal or time-series geospatial data. Unlike traditional neural networks, RNNs have connections that loop back on themselves, allowing them to maintain information about previous time steps. This makes them particularly effective for modeling data with temporal dependencies, such as satellite time-series data or climate change predictions.

2.7.1 Structure of RNN

- **Input Layer**: Takes sequential data over time, such as a series of satellite images taken at different times or sensor readings recorded at intervals.
- **Hidden Layers**: In an RNN, the hidden state from the previous time step is passed along to the current time step, allowing the network to learn from both past and present data.
- **Output Layer**: Produces the predicted output at each time step, such as the classification of land cover for each time point or the predicted future temperature.

2.7.2 Working Principle

RNNs work by maintaining a memory of previous time steps, enabling them to model temporal dependencies. Each unit in the hidden layer receives the input at time step t and the hidden state from time step $t - 1$. The hidden state is updated using an activation function (like tanh or ReLU), and the output is based on the hidden state at each time step. The looped structure allows RNNs to capture long-term dependencies in the data.

2.7.3 Types of RNNs

- **Vanilla RNNs**: Basic RNNs that process sequences step by step, passing information from one time step to the next.
- **LSTM (Long Short-Term Memory)**: A specialized RNN that is capable of learning long-term dependencies by solving the vanishing gradient problem, making it suitable for handling sequences with long-range temporal dependencies.
- **GRU (Gated Recurrent Units)**: A simplified version of LSTM that is computationally more efficient while retaining the ability to capture long-term dependencies.

2.7.4 Applications in Geospatial Domain

RNNs, especially LSTMs and GRUs, are well-suited for analyzing temporal patterns in geospatial data. Some common applications include:

- **Crop Phenology Modeling**: Predicting the growth stages of crops over time based on satellite observations.
- **Flood Prediction**: Modeling rainfall and river flow data over time to forecast flood events.

- **Climate Trend Analysis**: Detecting long-term climate changes by analyzing time-series data of temperature, precipitation, and other environmental variables.
- **Drought Monitoring**: Predicting drought conditions by analyzing seasonal weather patterns and vegetation indices over time.

2.7.5 Advantages and Limitations

Advantages:

- Can capture temporal dependencies and trends in geospatial data.
- Suitable for applications involving time-series satellite images, climate data, or sensor data.
- LSTMs and GRUs are robust to long-range dependencies, making them more effective for tasks like seasonal analysis and trend forecasting.

Limitations:

- Vanilla RNNs suffer from the vanishing gradient problem, making them less effective for very long sequences.
- Training RNNs, particularly LSTMs and GRUs, can be computationally intensive.
- RNNs may struggle with spatial data, necessitating hybrid architectures that combine RNNs with CNNs for spatial-temporal analysis.

2.8 Deep Learning Workflow for Geospatial Tasks

The application of deep learning to geospatial tasks involves several stages, from data acquisition to deployment. Each step is crucial to ensure the successful development of a deep learning model that can accurately process and analyze geospatial data. The workflow can be broken down into the following four key stages:

2.8.1 Data Acquisition and Preprocessing

The first step in any deep learning project is to acquire relevant geospatial data. This can include satellite imagery, aerial photographs, LiDAR data, and other forms of spatial data. The data must be gathered from reliable sources such as remote sensing platforms, GIS repositories, or sensor networks. Once acquired, the data undergoes preprocessing, which is essential for ensuring the quality and consistency of the data. Preprocessing tasks include:

- **Data cleaning:** Removing noise, correcting errors, and handling missing data.
- **Data normalization:** Scaling pixel values, or adjusting features to a uniform range.

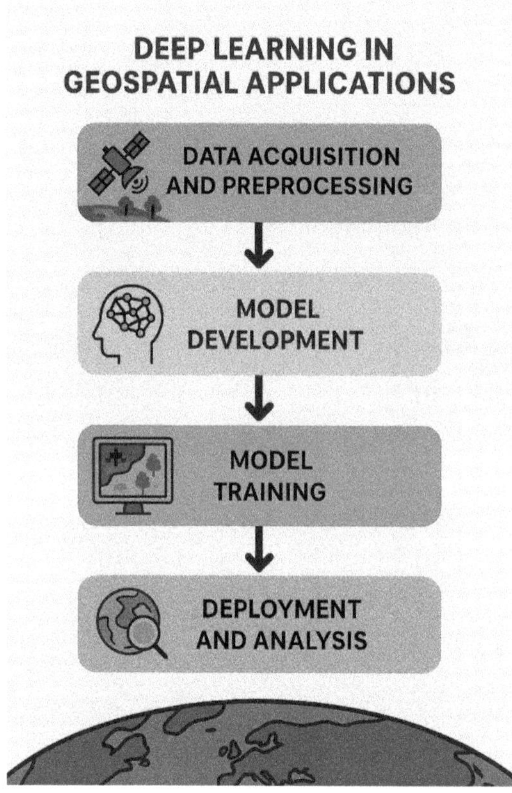

Figure 2.3: Deep Learning Workflow for Geospatial Tasks

- **Data augmentation:** Applying transformations like rotation, scaling, and flipping to increase the diversity of the dataset.
- **Data labeling:** Annotating geospatial data with the correct labels (e.g., land cover types, vegetation, etc.) for supervised learning.

2.8.2 Model Development

Once the data is prepared, the next step is to design the deep learning model. This involves choosing the appropriate architecture based on the nature of the task. For geospatial tasks, commonly used architectures include:

- **Multilayer Perceptrons (MLP):** For simpler tasks where spatial dependencies are not critical.
- **Convolutional Neural Networks (CNN):** Particularly useful for image-based tasks such as land cover classification or object detection.
- **Recurrent Neural Networks (RNN):** Effective for temporal geospatial data, such as

modeling dynamic changes in land use or vegetation over time.

- **Generative Adversarial Networks (GAN):** Used for tasks like image enhancement, data generation, or data synthesis from limited samples.

The model development phase also involves selecting the loss function, optimization algorithms, and regularization techniques to prevent overfitting.

2.8.3 Model Training

Training a deep learning model involves feeding the prepared data into the model, adjusting the model's parameters (weights), and minimizing the loss function. This phase is computationally intensive and requires powerful hardware such as GPUs or TPUs. Key steps include:

- **Splitting the dataset:** Dividing the data into training, validation, and test sets.
- **Hyperparameter tuning:** Adjusting learning rates, batch sizes, and other parameters to optimize model performance.
- **Model evaluation:** Evaluating the model's performance on the validation set using metrics such as accuracy, F1-score, or Intersection over Union (IoU) for segmentation tasks.
- **Model validation:** Ensuring that the model does not overfit by evaluating on a held-out validation set.

2.8.4 Deployment and Analysis

After training, the model is deployed to make predictions on new, unseen geospatial data. The deployment process involves integrating the model into a user-friendly application or system, such as a GIS or a remote sensing analysis tool. The model's output can then be used to generate actionable insights for decision-making in fields like urban planning, environmental monitoring, agriculture, or disaster management. Key considerations during deployment include:

- **Model optimization:** Reducing model size or computation time for faster predictions (e.g., using quantization or pruning techniques).
- **Real-time inference:** Deploying models in real-time applications, such as monitoring vegetation growth or tracking changes in urban development.
- **Post-deployment analysis:** Monitoring the performance of the model in real-world applications, adjusting as necessary, and continuously improving the model with new data.

This phase is crucial for ensuring that the model remains accurate and effective over time as new data becomes available.

2.9 Deep Learning Frameworks for Geospatial Developers

The success of deep learning in geospatial applications heavily depends on the availability of powerful and flexible frameworks. These frameworks simplify the model building, training, and deployment processes while offering domain-specific utilities tailored for geospatial data.

- **TensorFlow & Keras:** TensorFlow, developed by Google, is a comprehensive deep learning framework that supports both low-level operations and high-level model building. Keras, which is integrated into TensorFlow, offers a user-friendly API that simplifies model prototyping and experimentation. Together, they are particularly effective for building and deploying deep learning models in production environments with support for multi-GPU training, TensorBoard visualization, and model optimization.
- **PyTorch:** PyTorch, developed by Facebook's AI Research lab, is widely favored in the research community due to its dynamic computation graph, which provides greater flexibility during model development. It allows for intuitive debugging and supports a Pythonic programming style, making it suitable for iterative and experimental research in deep learning for geospatial analytics.
- **FastAI:** Built on top of PyTorch, FastAI offers high-level abstractions that make it easy to train state-of-the-art deep learning models with minimal code. It includes support for transfer learning and offers specialized tools for working with image, text, and tabular data. For geospatial developers, FastAI's seamless integration with PyTorch enables quick adaptation for satellite image classification and segmentation tasks.

Specialized Libraries

In addition to general-purpose deep learning frameworks, several libraries are tailored to address the unique needs of geospatial data processing:

- **torchgeo:** A PyTorch-based library developed to simplify working with geospatial raster and vector data. It includes dataset classes for commonly used satellite products, utilities for georeferenced data handling, and integration with spatial transforms and sampling strategies. This makes it ideal for remote sensing tasks like land cover classification and change detection.
- **segmentation_models_pytorch:** This library provides a collection of pre-trained encoder-decoder architectures (like U-Net, FPN, LinkNet) specifically designed for image segmentation tasks. It is highly useful for tasks such as building footprint extraction,

road detection, and waterbody segmentation from satellite imagery.

- **eo-learn:** An open-source Python library for processing spatiotemporal Earth observation (EO) data, eo-learn provides utilities for working with Sentinel-2 and Landsat time-series data. It enables the construction of reusable EO workflows including cloud masking, vegetation index computation, and temporal feature extraction, all of which are essential for agricultural and environmental monitoring.
- **rastervision:** Raster Vision is a deep learning framework for aerial and satellite imagery developed by Azavea. It supports training, evaluating, and deploying models for object detection, classification, and semantic segmentation. Its modular pipeline and cloud-compatibility make it suitable for large-scale geospatial data processing and deployment.

2.10 Geospatial Model Evaluation Metrics

Evaluating the performance of deep learning models in geospatial applications requires the use of specific metrics that align with the task type and spatial context. Below is a categorized overview of the commonly used evaluation metrics in geospatial deep learning tasks:

2.10.1 Classification Tasks

For tasks such as land cover classification or object detection, the following metrics are widely used:

- **Accuracy:** The proportion of correctly predicted samples out of the total predictions. It is suitable when the dataset is balanced.
- **Precision:** Measures the proportion of true positives among all predicted positives. It is crucial when false positives are costly (e.g., detecting urban expansion).
- **Recall:** The proportion of true positives detected among all actual positives. It is useful in scenarios where missing a class (e.g., detecting disaster-affected areas) is problematic.
- **F1-Score:** The harmonic mean of precision and recall. It balances the trade-off between the two and is helpful when classes are imbalanced.

2.10.2 Segmentation Tasks

These tasks involve pixel-wise classification, such as building footprint extraction or vegetation cover mapping:

- **Intersection over Union (IoU):** Also known as the Jaccard Index, it measures the overlap between the predicted and ground truth segmentation areas. It is a critical metric for object localization in geospatial imagery.

Table 2.2: Comparison of Evaluation Metrics for Geospatial Deep Learning Tasks

Metric	Applicable Task	Description
Accuracy	Classification	Proportion of correctly classified samples over the total samples.
Precision	Classification	Ratio of true positives to predicted positives; highlights false positives.
Recall	Classification	Ratio of true positives to actual positives; important when missing instances is costly.
F1-Score	Classification	Harmonic mean of precision and recall; useful for imbalanced datasets.
IoU (Jaccard Index)	Segmentation	Measures the overlap between predicted and ground truth regions.
Dice Coefficient	Segmentation	Similar to IoU, emphasizes agreement between predicted and actual segmentation masks.
RMSE	Regression	Square root of average squared prediction errors; penalizes large errors.
MAE	Regression	Average of absolute differences between predictions and actual values.
Area Agreement	Spatial-specific	Evaluates agreement between predicted and actual spatial extents.
Boundary Accuracy	Spatial-specific	Measures how accurately boundaries of spatial features are delineated.

- **Dice Coefficient:** Similar to IoU but slightly more sensitive to small object detection. It is particularly used in medical and remote sensing image segmentation.

2.10.3 Regression Tasks

These metrics are used in continuous value predictions, such as estimating temperature or NDVI values:

- **Root Mean Square Error (RMSE):** Evaluates the square root of the average squared difference between predicted and actual values. It penalizes larger errors more heavily and is suitable for precise measurements.
- **Mean Absolute Error (MAE):** Computes the average absolute difference between predictions and ground truth, providing a more interpretable measure of average error magnitude.

2.10.4 Spatial-Specific Metrics

In geospatial applications, spatial accuracy is as important as statistical accuracy:

- **Area Agreement:** Measures how closely the predicted spatial extent of classes (e.g., forest, water) matches the reference data. This is crucial in tasks like land cover change detection.

- **Boundary Accuracy:** Assesses how well the model delineates the edges or boundaries of spatial features such as coastlines, rivers, or building perimeters. This metric becomes essential when fine-grained spatial detail is required.

2.11 Challenges and Considerations in Geospatial Deep Learning

Deep learning applications in geospatial data face several unique challenges that need to be addressed to ensure robust, accurate, and effective model performance. These challenges are inherent to the nature of geospatial data and must be considered throughout the model development lifecycle. The primary challenges include:

(1) **Data Scarcity**
- **Problem:** One of the biggest hurdles in geospatial deep learning is the limited availability of labeled geospatial datasets. Unlike other domains like image classification or speech recognition, acquiring high-quality, labeled geospatial data is often a time-consuming and expensive process. Satellite imagery and other geospatial data types require expert knowledge to accurately annotate, making it difficult to create large, labeled datasets for training models.
- **Impact:** The lack of sufficient labeled data can lead to poor model performance, overfitting, or bias. In addition, data scarcity makes it hard to build robust models that generalize well across different geospatial regions.

(2) **Class Imbalance**
- **Problem:** In many geospatial tasks, especially land-use/land-cover (LULC) mapping, there is often a significant class imbalance. For instance, the number of urban areas in a satellite image may be much smaller than the number of forested or agricultural areas. This class imbalance can cause the model to favor the more frequent class, leading to inaccurate predictions, especially for the minority class.
- **Impact:** Class imbalance results in biased model predictions and poor performance, particularly in terms of detecting underrepresented classes like urban areas, water bodies, or rare vegetation types.

(3) **Clouds and Shadows**
- **Problem:** Optical remote sensing data, such as satellite imagery, is frequently affected by clouds and shadows, which obscure the ground surface. These obstructions introduce significant noise into the data, making it difficult for models to accurately analyze features of interest, particularly in regions with frequent cloud cover.

- **Impact:** Clouds and shadows can lead to missing or incorrect information, complicating tasks like vegetation mapping, land cover classification, and disaster monitoring. The challenge is further compounded in regions with seasonal variations in cloud cover, which can change the availability of clear imagery.

(4) **Computational Load**

- **Problem:** Deep learning models, especially convolutional neural networks (CNNs) and recurrent neural networks (RNNs), are computationally intensive. Training these models on large geospatial datasets requires significant computational resources, often including high-performance GPUs. The demand for such resources can limit access to deep learning capabilities for researchers and developers with less computing power.

- **Impact:** Long training times and the need for specialized hardware (like GPUs or TPUs) can create barriers to entry for researchers and organizations with limited computational resources. Additionally, the high computational cost may hinder experimentation and rapid prototyping.

(5) **Generalization**

- **Problem:** Geospatial data is often highly region-specific due to the variability in climate, topography, vegetation types, and urbanization patterns across different geographic locations. A model trained on data from one region may not generalize well to another due to these spatial differences. This is particularly challenging when transferring models trained in one part of the world to regions with different characteristics.

- **Impact:** The inability to generalize across different geographies can result in poor model performance, as the trained model may not adapt to the spatial variability present in new regions. This issue is especially problematic in applications like land cover classification or vegetation mapping, where local context is critical.

Summary

This chapter provided an introduction to deep learning and its applications in geospatial data analysis. We explored the foundational concepts of deep learning, including key architectures such as **Multilayer Perceptrons (MLP)**, **Convolutional Neural Networks (CNNs)**, and **Recurrent Neural Networks (RNNs)**, focusing on how these models are applied to various geospatial tasks like image classification, land cover mapping, and time-series analysis of satellite data.

We also covered the **deep learning workflow** specific to geospatial applications, emphasizing data acquisition, preprocessing, model development, training, and deployment. Several popular deep learning frameworks were discussed, including **TensorFlow**, **PyTorch**, and

FastAI, with a special focus on domain-specific libraries like **torchgeo** and **rastervision**.

Additionally, we looked at **model evaluation metrics** tailored to geospatial tasks such as accuracy, precision, recall for classification, and Intersection over Union (IoU) for segmentation. The chapter concluded with an overview of the challenges faced when applying deep learning to geospatial problems, such as data scarcity, class imbalance, and computational constraints.

In summary, deep learning provides powerful tools for geospatial data analysis, but its application requires careful consideration of data quality, model choice, and computational resources.

Exercise Questions

(1) Explain why deep learning is well-suited for geospatial intelligence applications.
(2) Compare and contrast the different types of activation functions.
(3) Describe how transfer learning can be beneficial when working with geospatial data.
(4) Explain the differences between MLP, CNN, and RNN. Provide examples of geospatial applications for each model.
(5) What are the key steps involved in the deep learning workflow for geospatial tasks? Describe the importance of each step.
(6) Discuss the challenges of applying deep learning to geospatial data. How can data scarcity and class imbalance be addressed in model training?
(7) What are the main evaluation metrics for classification and segmentation tasks in geospatial deep learning? How do these metrics impact model performance?
(8) Why is the generalization of deep learning models across different geographic regions challenging? Provide strategies to address this issue.
(9) What are some specialized libraries for geospatial deep learning? Discuss the role of libraries like torchgeo, segmentation_models_pytorch, and rastervision.
(10) How does GPU acceleration benefit deep learning in geospatial applications? Discuss the computational challenges and solutions for large geospatial datasets.

Notes and Suggestions

- **Practical Application:** For those new to deep learning, it is recommended to start by experimenting with smaller datasets, such as those available in **Google Earth Engine** or **Sentinel Hub**. These platforms offer accessible geospatial datasets that can help you get hands-on experience with deep learning models.

- **Data Preprocessing:** Pay close attention to preprocessing steps. Geospatial data often comes with noise (clouds, shadows, etc.) and requires significant cleaning and normalization. Explore techniques like data augmentation to improve model robustness.
- **Model Selection:** While CNNs are typically used for image-based tasks, RNNs are beneficial when handling temporal geospatial data, such as land use change over time. Understanding the strengths and weaknesses of each model is key to successful application.
- **Experimentation:** Given the computational intensity of deep learning models, experiment with smaller versions of models first, and scale them up as you gather more computational resources. Many cloud platforms provide GPU acceleration on a pay-per-use basis, which can significantly reduce training times.
- **Stay Updated:** Deep learning frameworks and libraries are constantly evolving. Keep an eye on the latest research papers, conferences, and updates from platforms like **arXiv** or **GitHub** to stay informed about new techniques and tools in the geospatial domain.
- **Integration with GIS Tools:** Combining deep learning with traditional GIS tools like **QGIS** or **ArcGIS** can be powerful. Use deep learning models for feature extraction or predictive analysis and then apply them within the GIS platform for further visualization and analysis.

Chapter 3

Ethical and Practical Challenges in Geospatial AI

Learning Objectives

At the end of this chapter, you should be able to:

- Understand key ethical considerations in using AI with geospatial data
- Identify practical challenges in working with large-scale spatial datasets
- Discuss issues of bias, privacy, and data fairness
- Explore strategies to mitigate ethical and technical risks

3.1 Introduction

As deep learning is increasingly applied to geospatial data, ethical and practical concerns have emerged that demand attention from both researchers and practitioners. This chapter outlines some of the core challenges—including data privacy, algorithmic bias, reproducibility, and responsible model deployment—especially when applied to societal applications like urban planning, disaster response, or surveillance.

3.2 Data Privacy and Geospatial Ethics

Geospatial data often includes sensitive or personally identifiable information, especially when derived from mobile devices, drones, or high-resolution satellite imagery. Violations of location privacy can have serious consequences, from political surveillance to unintended exposure of marginalized communities.

3.2.1 Examples of Privacy Risks

- High-resolution imagery revealing private property
- Public datasets with embedded personal identifiers
- Tracking individuals through anonymized mobility data

Best Practices:

- Use anonymized and aggregated data wherever possible
- Follow local and international data governance laws (e.g., GDPR)
- Apply differential privacy or spatial masking techniques

3.3 Bias in Geospatial Datasets

Bias in training data can lead to unfair or inaccurate models. This may arise from under-representation of certain geographic regions, seasonal imbalance, or social and cultural blind spots.

Sources of Bias:

- Urban-biased datasets excluding rural or tribal regions
- Seasonal variations not represented in time-series data
- Annotated datasets with inconsistent labeling

Mitigation Strategies:

- Ensure dataset diversity across space and time
- Use stratified sampling and active learning
- Conduct fairness audits of model outputs

3.4 Reproducibility and Openness

Reproducibility in spatial AI requires transparent sharing of data, models, and code. However, proprietary software, restricted datasets, or unlogged preprocessing can hinder replication.

Recommendations:

- Publish data and code with proper documentation
- Use open platforms (e.g., GitHub, Zenodo, Earth Engine Apps)
- Include random seeds and hardware specs in experiments

3.5 Environmental Considerations

Training deep neural networks can be computationally expensive and carbon-intensive, especially with large remote sensing datasets.

Suggestions:

- Use efficient architectures (e.g., MobileNet, quantized models)
- Prefer transfer learning over training from scratch
- Consider carbon offsets or green data centers

3.6 Ethical Deployment of Models

Even well-trained models can be misused or interpreted out of context when deployed without safeguards.

Checklist for Responsible Deployment:

- Are the users trained to interpret model outputs?
- Is the model updated as new data becomes available?
- Are the limitations and assumptions clearly communicated?

Summary

- Ethical challenges in geospatial AI include data privacy, bias, reproducibility, and ecological footprint.
- Practical solutions involve adopting open science practices, fairness audits, and environmental accountability.

Exercise Questions

(1) Explain how location data can lead to privacy breaches. Give two mitigation strategies.

(2) What types of biases might be present in satellite image classification datasets?

(3) Discuss how reproducibility can be promoted in deep geospatial models.

(4) List three environmental concerns of using deep learning in geospatial applications.

Notes and Suggestions

- Encourage students to explore ethical AI guidelines from organizations like the OECD, AI Now Institute, and Partnership on AI.
- Consider hosting a debate or case study discussion around controversial geospatial applications.

Part II

Methodologies and Tools

Chapter 4

Software Stack for Geospatial Deep Learning

Learning Objectives

At the end of this chapter, you should be able to:

- Understand the core software tools used in geospatial deep learning.
- Explore the roles of programming languages, GIS platforms, and cloud services in geospatial data processing.
- Gain familiarity with key libraries for raster data handling and deep learning model development.
- Learn hardware and software requirements for efficient workflow in geospatial deep learning.

4.1 Introduction

Geospatial deep learning is revolutionizing fields such as land cover classification, disaster risk assessment, and environmental monitoring by combining spatial data analysis with cutting-edge machine learning techniques. These applications require sophisticated software stacks that seamlessly integrate geospatial tools, deep learning frameworks, and cloud services. The challenge lies not only in understanding the technologies but also in efficiently implementing them for real-world applications. This chapter provides a detailed overview of essential software tools that form a geospatial deep learning pipeline, focusing on open-source

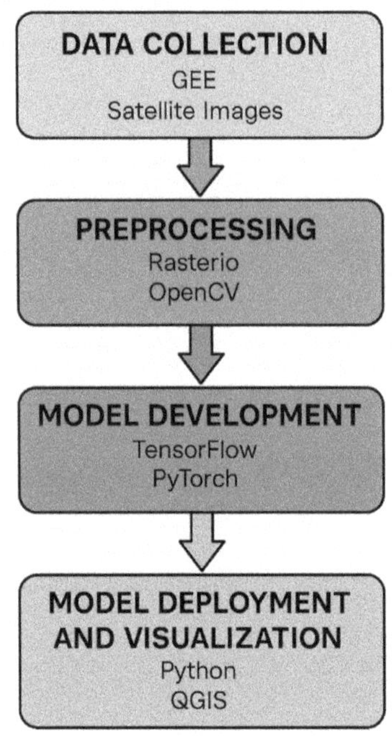

Figure 4.1: Software Stack Pipeline for Geospatial Deep Learning

platforms, cloud services, and libraries that have proven effective in research and practical applications.

4.2 Programming Language: Python

Python has become the de facto language for geospatial deep learning due to its flexibility, rich libraries, and ease of use. Whether you are preprocessing satellite imagery or building a deep learning model, Python provides a unified ecosystem for both.

4.2.1 Why Python?

- **Ease of Learning:** Python's syntax resembles natural language, making it highly accessible for newcomers.
- **Rich Libraries:** Python hosts an extensive collection of libraries such as TensorFlow, PyTorch, Rasterio, and Geopandas.

- **Community Resources:** With a global user base, Python benefits from a plethora of tutorials, forums, and open-source contributions.
- **Integration:** Python can seamlessly integrate with GIS software, cloud platforms, and other languages (e.g., C/C++) for optimized performance.

Example: Python scripts can automate workflows such as extracting vegetation indices (e.g., NDVI) from satellite images using libraries like Rasterio and Geopandas, which are then fed into Convolutional Neural Networks (CNNs) built in TensorFlow for land cover classification.

Pro Tip: Always work within a `virtual environment` using `venv` or `conda` to isolate dependencies and avoid version conflicts between libraries.

4.3 Desktop GIS Platform: QGIS

QGIS is one of the most powerful open-source geographic information systems, enabling the visualization, analysis, and manipulation of geospatial data. It is widely used in academic, governmental, and commercial sectors for a wide range of geospatial tasks.

4.3.1 Key Features

- **Multi-format Support:** Handles a variety of data types including raster, vector, and mesh datasets.
- **Spatial Analysis:** Provides tools for terrain modeling, hydrological analysis, and proximity analysis.
- **Customization:** Supports plugins and Python scripting via the PyQGIS API, allowing users to extend functionality.

Example: QGIS can be used to preprocess satellite images by reprojecting datasets, clipping rasters to areas of interest, and calculating terrain parameters such as slope, aspect, and elevation.

Pro Tip: Use the QGIS Processing Toolbox for automation of repetitive tasks like raster clipping and band calculations. It helps reduce human error and improves workflow efficiency.

4.4 Cloud Platform: Google Earth Engine (GEE)

Google Earth Engine is a powerful cloud-based platform that enables the processing of geospatial data at scale. It is particularly beneficial for large-scale temporal analysis of satellite data, offering access to vast archives of imagery and geospatial datasets.

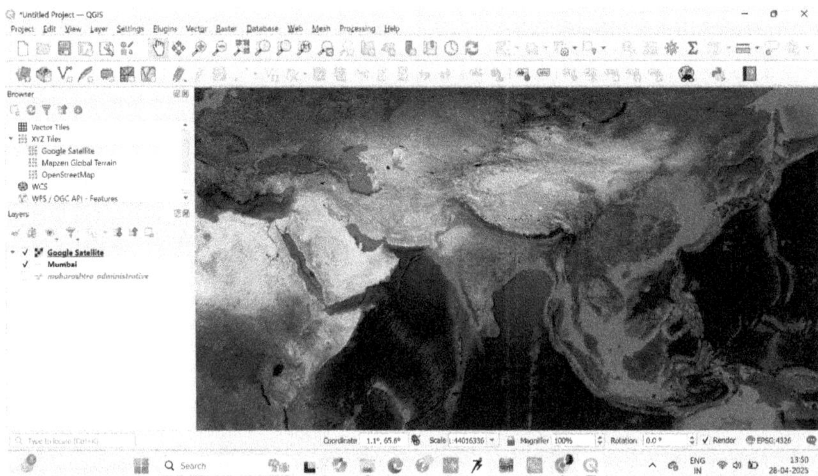

Figure 4.2: Sample QGIS Interface Used for Preprocessing Satellite Data

4.4.1   Advantages of GEE

- **Massive Data Archive:** Access to vast libraries of satellite imagery, climate data, and more, spanning decades.
- **Cloud Computing:** GEE eliminates the need for expensive hardware by providing cloud-based processing.
- **APIs for Analysis:** Supports JavaScript and Python APIs for custom algorithm development.

Example: GEE is widely used to create cloud-free composite images over large geographic regions, enabling time series analysis of land cover changes. For instance, monitoring deforestation trends over a 20-year period in the Amazon rainforest.

Pro Tip: When using GEE for time-series analysis, always check for cloud cover and atmospheric interference in your image composites. GEE's built-in filters can help, but manual inspection is crucial.

4.5   Proprietary Alternatives of GIS Tools

While open-source GIS tools like QGIS, Google Earth Engine, and others are widely used in the geospatial community, several proprietary tools offer advanced features, enterprise-level support, and more polished user interfaces. These proprietary tools are often preferred by large organizations, commercial enterprises, and governments for their robustness, customer support, and integrated solutions. Below is an overview of some of the most popular proprietary GIS tools and their applications.

4.5.1 ArcGIS by Esri

ArcGIS is one of the most widely used GIS platforms in commercial, governmental, and industrial applications. It is a comprehensive suite of tools for mapping, spatial analysis, data management, and geospatial application development.

4.5.1.1 Key Features

- **Advanced Spatial Analysis:** ArcGIS provides sophisticated tools for spatial analysis, including tools for geostatistics, 3D modeling, and geospatial data interpolation.
- **Rich Data Integration:** ArcGIS supports multiple data formats, such as shapefiles, GeoJSON, and raster datasets, and integrates easily with other enterprise systems.
- **Geoprocessing Tools:** The platform includes a wide array of built-in geoprocessing tools for data manipulation, transformation, and analysis.
- **Cloud Integration:** ArcGIS can integrate with cloud platforms for large-scale data storage, processing, and collaboration.

4.5.1.2 Example Application

ArcGIS is commonly used for urban planning and infrastructure management. For example, cities often use ArcGIS for detailed land use analysis, transportation planning, and managing public utilities.

Pro Tip: ArcGIS users often face challenges when dealing with large datasets. It is advisable to utilize the ArcGIS Pro's "Raster Functions" for on-the-fly processing to optimize performance when working with large raster datasets.

4.5.2 ERDAS IMAGINE

ERDAS IMAGINE is a leading GIS tool designed for raster data processing and remote sensing applications. It is used for data analysis, mapping, and model building.

4.5.2.1 Key Features

- **Image Processing:** ERDAS IMAGINE excels at image processing tasks such as radiometric and geometric correction, enhancement, and image classification.
- **Modeling and Simulation:** The platform offers a range of modeling tools for spatial data analysis and environmental simulation.

- **LiDAR Data Processing:** ERDAS IMAGINE provides tools for working with LiDAR data, including terrain modeling, vegetation analysis, and 3D visualization.
- **Advanced Image Classification:** Supports both supervised and unsupervised classification methods, making it suitable for land cover classification and change detection.

4.5.2.2 Example Application

ERDAS IMAGINE is used extensively in environmental monitoring, such as deforestation detection, agricultural monitoring, and water quality assessment using satellite imagery. Its powerful image classification tools make it ideal for applications like detecting crop health or forest cover.

Pro Tip: For users working with LiDAR data, ERDAS IMAGINE provides excellent tools for filtering and classifying point clouds, which is essential for accurate terrain modeling and feature extraction.

4.5.3 MapInfo Professional

MapInfo Professional is a desktop GIS software used for mapping, spatial analysis, and visualization. It is particularly popular in business analytics and urban planning applications due to its ease of use and integration with business intelligence tools.

4.5.3.1 Key Features

- **Data Visualization:** MapInfo provides a user-friendly interface for creating thematic maps and visualizing complex geospatial data.
- **Business Analytics Integration:** MapInfo allows integration with business intelligence tools for spatial analysis of market data, demographics, and customer segmentation.
- **3D Visualization:** The software supports 3D visualization for urban modeling, terrain mapping, and infrastructure management.
- **Customization:** MapInfo offers powerful customization options through its scripting and extension capabilities.

4.5.3.2 Example Application

MapInfo Professional is commonly used by businesses for market analysis, logistics optimization, and customer segmentation. It is also used in urban planning for zoning analysis and infrastructure management.

Pro Tip: MapInfo's "Geocoding" tool can help businesses map customer addresses onto their geospatial data for targeted market analysis. However, it is crucial to clean the address data before geocoding to ensure accurate results.

4.5.4 Global Mapper

Global Mapper is a versatile GIS software known for its intuitive interface and advanced data processing capabilities. It is particularly effective for users who need to work with large datasets, 3D terrain data, and lidar point clouds.

4.5.4.1 Key Features

- **3D Terrain Visualization:** Global Mapper offers advanced 3D visualization tools for terrain analysis, urban modeling, and resource management.
- **Multi-format Support:** It supports a wide range of data formats, including raster, vector, and LiDAR data, making it suitable for diverse geospatial applications.
- **Analysis and Conversion:** Global Mapper includes tools for spatial analysis, terrain modeling, and data conversion between different formats.
- **LiDAR Processing:** The software provides robust tools for working with LiDAR point clouds, including classification, filtering, and 3D feature extraction.

4.5.4.2 Example Application

Global Mapper is used in natural resource management, including forestry and mining, where 3D terrain modeling and LiDAR point cloud analysis are crucial. It is also used for infrastructure planning, such as road design and flood modeling.

Pro Tip: When dealing with large LiDAR datasets in Global Mapper, it's recommended to first filter and classify the point clouds to reduce data size and improve processing speed.

4.5.5 Proprietary Alternatives for Cloud GIS: Autodesk InfraWorks and Bentley Systems

For large-scale, enterprise-level geospatial analysis and infrastructure modeling, proprietary cloud-based GIS tools like Autodesk InfraWorks and Bentley Systems are widely used.

4.5.5.1 Autodesk InfraWorks

Autodesk InfraWorks is a comprehensive tool for infrastructure design and modeling. It integrates with other Autodesk tools, such as AutoCAD and Revit, to provide end-to-end solutions for transportation, urban planning, and environmental modeling.

Pro Tip: InfraWorks' ability to handle 3D city modeling makes it a great tool for urban planners. When using this tool, always ensure that your 3D models are up-to-date to maintain the accuracy of your visualizations and analyses.

4.5.5.2 Bentley Systems

Bentley Systems offers advanced solutions for civil engineering, construction, and infrastructure planning. Its tools, such as MicroStation and OpenCities, provide robust capabilities for geospatial modeling, asset management, and civil engineering analysis.

Pro Tip: For large-scale infrastructure projects, Bentley Systems provides tools that seamlessly integrate with GIS databases, making it easier to manage project data and maintain up-to-date records throughout the lifecycle of the infrastructure.

Table 4.1: Comparison of Free and Open-Source vs Proprietary GIS Software

Aspect	Free and Open-Source GIS Software (e.g., QGIS, Google Earth Engine)	Proprietary GIS Software (e.g., ArcGIS, ERDAS IMAGINE, MapInfo)
Cost	Free to use, no licensing fees.	Expensive licensing, subscription, or annual fees.
Customization and Flexibility	Highly customizable, with access to source code for modifications.	Limited customization; closed-source with restrictions.
Community Support	Strong community-driven support via forums, online resources, etc.	Professional support from vendors, but often requires a subscription.
Features	May have fewer advanced features or require third-party plugins.	Comprehensive, highly polished features with advanced tools for professional use.
Data Compatibility	Supports a wide variety of formats, but may require plugins for some formats.	Seamless integration with proprietary data formats and enterprise systems.
Updates and Improvements	Frequent updates from the community, but may lack a formal support timeline.	Regular updates with formal support and long-term roadmap.
Usability	Can have steeper learning curve, especially for beginners.	User-friendly interfaces with better documentation and tutorials.
Integration with Other Software	Integrates well with open-source tools but may face challenges with proprietary systems.	Excellent integration with other enterprise software like CAD, databases, and business intelligence tools.
Deployment and Scaling	Can be deployed freely on any system, but scalability might be limited depending on hardware.	Designed for enterprise deployment, capable of handling large-scale operations with robust scaling solutions.
Security	Open-source, meaning anyone can inspect and contribute to security, but may require vigilance from users.	Security protocols are managed by the vendor, often with regular security patches.
Licensing and Legal Considerations	No licensing restrictions; completely open for use and modification.	Licensing agreements may restrict usage, and there may be concerns with vendor lock-in.
Collaboration and Sharing	Easy sharing with other open-source systems and datasets.	Collaboration may be restricted by proprietary file formats or software versions.

4.6 Key Deep Learning Libraries

Deep learning is integral to many geospatial applications. Libraries such as TensorFlow and PyTorch enable researchers to build, train, and deploy advanced models for image classification, segmentation, and prediction tasks.

4.6.1 TensorFlow

TensorFlow is one of the most widely used deep learning frameworks, developed by Google. It provides a comprehensive ecosystem for building and deploying machine learning models, particularly in computer vision.

- **Ease of Model Building:** The Keras API simplifies the process of model prototyping, while TensorFlow provides tools for production-level deployment.
- **GPU Acceleration:** TensorFlow offers support for distributed training across GPUs and TPUs, enabling faster model development.
- **Production Ready:** TensorFlow Serving and TensorFlow Lite help deploy models to cloud platforms or mobile devices.

Example: TensorFlow has been applied extensively in Land Use Land Cover (LULC) classification. Researchers use CNNs to classify satellite imagery into distinct land cover types like water, vegetation, and urban areas, which can aid in environmental monitoring and urban planning.

Pro Tip: When working with large datasets in TensorFlow, consider using `tf.data` API to efficiently handle data pipelines, reducing memory overhead during training.

4.6.2 PyTorch

PyTorch, developed by Facebook, is known for its flexibility and ease of use, making it especially popular in academic research.

- **Dynamic Computation Graphs:** PyTorch uses a dynamic (define-by-run) approach, which is great for debugging and rapid experimentation.
- **Rich Ecosystem:** It includes libraries for advanced applications such as graph neural networks and sequence modeling.
- **Strong Research Support:** The research community contributes heavily to PyTorch, making it easy to access cutting-edge developments.

Example: PyTorch is commonly used for object detection in satellite imagery. U-Net models, often used for pixel-wise segmentation tasks, can be trained using PyTorch to detect buildings, roads, or flood-affected areas in remotely sensed images.

Table 4.2: Comparison between TensorFlow and PyTorch for Geospatial Deep Learning

Feature	TensorFlow	PyTorch
Ease of Use	Higher-level APIs like Keras make it easier for beginners.	More flexible and intuitive for researchers and developers.
Dynamic vs Static Graph	Static computation graph (TensorFlow 1.x); Eager execution in TensorFlow 2.x.	Dynamic computation graph (define-by-run approach).
Community Support	Extensive industrial support (e.g., Google, production-grade deployments).	Strong academic and research support (frequent in papers).
Geospatial Applications	LULC classification, segmentation tasks using CNNs.	Temporal analysis, graph-based spatial learning (e.g., using PyTorch Geometric).
Integration with GEE	Supported through TensorFlow Earth Engine integration.	Can use exported GEE datasets, needs manual integration.

4.7 Geospatial Data Handling Libraries

Handling raster and vector data is a core task in geospatial deep learning workflows. Libraries like Rasterio and OpenCV provide essential functionality for reading, processing, and augmenting satellite imagery.

4.7.1 Rasterio

Rasterio is a powerful Python library for reading and writing raster data, enabling easy manipulation of geospatial image formats such as GeoTIFF.

- **Simple I/O Operations:** Reads and writes various raster formats, including GeoTIFF and JPEG2000.
- **CRS Management:** Rasterio can reproject raster data between different coordinate reference systems (CRS), ensuring accurate alignment.
- **Integration with Numpy:** Raster data can be treated as Numpy arrays, making it compatible with many scientific libraries.

Example: Rasterio is used to extract a region of interest (ROI) from a large satellite image and to apply basic analysis, such as calculating vegetation indices (NDVI), which are often used in environmental monitoring and land cover classification.

4.7.2   OpenCV

Originally developed for computer vision tasks, OpenCV has become a popular tool for image processing in the geospatial domain. Its capabilities for image enhancement, filtering, and object detection are invaluable for satellite image preprocessing.

- **Preprocessing:** OpenCV provides tools for denoising, contrast stretching, and histogram equalization, improving the quality of satellite imagery.
- **Data Augmentation:** OpenCV's image manipulation functions help create augmented datasets for model training, such as rotating or flipping images to simulate different viewpoints.
- **Feature Engineering:** Edge detection and contour analysis can help identify features such as roads and rivers in remote sensing imagery.

Example: OpenCV is applied in road extraction projects from high-resolution satellite imagery, enhancing feature boundaries before passing the data into deep learning models for classification.

4.8   Recommended Hardware for Geospatial Deep Learning

Students and researchers often wonder what hardware setup to use for geospatial deep learning tasks. While cloud platforms offer flexibility, local hardware is also critical for handling large datasets.

4.8.1   Minimum Specifications

- **Processor:** Intel i7 or AMD Ryzen 7 (Quad-core minimum)
- **Memory (RAM):** 16–32 GB recommended
- **GPU:** NVIDIA RTX 3060/3070 or higher (CUDA support)
- **Storage:** SSD with at least 512 GB capacity for faster data access

4.8.2   Cloud Alternatives

For users without powerful local machines, cloud platforms like Google Colab, AWS EC2, and Google Cloud AI offer scalable resources with GPU/TPU instances, enabling computational tasks without the need for high-end local hardware.

4.9   Summary

- Geospatial deep learning requires a well-integrated software stack, combining GIS tools, deep learning frameworks, and cloud platforms.
- Python is the core programming language for managing and processing geospatial data and developing deep learning models.
- QGIS and GEE are essential tools for spatial analysis and cloud-based data management.
- TensorFlow and PyTorch offer powerful platforms for deep learning model development, with specific strengths depending on the task.
- Rasterio and OpenCV are crucial for handling raster data, performing image preprocessing, and augmenting datasets.
- Proper hardware and cloud services are essential for training and deploying large-scale deep learning models in geospatial applications.

Exercise Questions

(1) Describe a typical workflow where Google Earth Engine and TensorFlow are used together.
(2) Explain the benefits of using Rasterio in preprocessing remote sensing data.
(3) Compare static versus dynamic computation graphs with examples.
(4) Suggest a personal hardware setup for students starting with geospatial deep learning.

Notes and Suggestions

- Practice by building simple pipelines combining QGIS and Python scripting.
- Explore open datasets available through Google Earth Engine for real-world project development.
- Start with simple CNN models in TensorFlow before advancing to architectures like U-Nets and GANs.
- Regularly document and back up coding projects using Git and cloud repositories.

Chapter 5

Model Validation and Accuracy Assessment

Learning Objectives

At the end of this chapter, you should be able to:

- Understand the importance of model validation in geospatial deep learning applications.
- Learn different techniques for model validation, including spatial k-fold cross-validation.
- Explore key metrics for assessing model performance, including F1-score, AUC-ROC, and Intersection over Union (IoU).
- Gain insight into how to interpret and apply these metrics to geospatial data.
- Understand the concept of overfitting and its implications for model validation.

5.1 Introduction

Model validation and accuracy assessment are crucial steps in the process of developing machine learning and deep learning models, particularly when the goal is to make reliable predictions from geospatial data. While training a model is essential, it is equally important to evaluate its performance using suitable techniques and metrics to ensure its effectiveness.

In geospatial deep learning, accuracy assessment involves evaluating how well a model performs in classifying, segmenting, or predicting spatial phenomena. Common tasks include land use land cover (LULC) classification, change detection, object detection, and environmental modeling. This chapter will provide an overview of various techniques and metrics used in the validation and assessment of models in geospatial contexts.

5.2 Importance of Model Validation in Geospatial Deep Learning

Model validation ensures that the trained model is not just memorizing the training data (i.e., overfitting) but is generalizable to unseen data. This is especially important in geospatial applications, where models are expected to handle complex spatial patterns and generalize to new geographic areas.

For example, in remote sensing tasks, such as classifying vegetation or identifying water bodies, a model must perform well not only on the specific regions in the training dataset but also on other, unseen regions. An incorrect or overfitted model could lead to inaccurate results and misinformed decision-making.

5.3 Spatial k-Fold Cross-Validation

Spatial k-fold cross-validation is a specific validation technique designed to account for the spatial structure in geospatial data. Unlike traditional k-fold cross-validation, where data is split randomly into training and validation sets, spatial k-fold ensures that the spatial relationships in the data are respected.

5.3.1 What is Spatial k-Fold Cross-Validation?

In spatial k-fold cross-validation, the dataset is divided into k spatially distinct subsets, such that each subset is geographically separated. The model is then trained on $k - 1$ of these subsets and tested on the remaining one. This process is repeated k times, with each subset serving as the validation set once.

5.3.2 Why is Spatial k-Fold Important?

In traditional k-fold cross-validation, random splits may cause data leakage, where data points in the training set are spatially close to those in the test set. In geospatial tasks, this spatial proximity can lead to overly optimistic performance estimates, as the model might exploit spatial autocorrelation rather than learning generalizable patterns. Spatial k-fold cross-validation addresses this issue by ensuring that the training and testing data do not overlap spatially, leading to more realistic performance metrics.

5.3.3 Example:

Consider a deep learning model that classifies land use from satellite imagery. The model could be trained on data from one region (e.g., urban areas) and tested on data from a different region (e.g., rural areas). This ensures that the model's ability to generalize across different geographic areas is tested, making the validation more robust.

5.4 Key Metrics for Model Evaluation

Once a model has been trained and validated, it is essential to measure its performance. This is where various metrics come into play. Below are some of the most commonly used metrics for evaluating geospatial models.

5.4.1 F1-Score

The F1-score is a widely used metric for assessing classification performance, especially when the dataset is imbalanced. It is the harmonic mean of precision and recall and provides a balance between the two.

$$F1 = 2 \times \frac{Precision \times Recall}{Precision + Recall}$$

Where:

$$Precision = \frac{TP}{TP + FP} \quad Recall = \frac{TP}{TP + FN}$$

- **True Positives (TP)**: Correctly predicted positive instances.
- **False Positives (FP)**: Incorrectly predicted as positive.
- **False Negatives (FN)**: Incorrectly predicted as negative.

5.4.2 AUC-ROC (Area Under the Curve - Receiver Operating Characteristic)

The AUC-ROC curve is another essential tool for evaluating binary classification models. It plots the true positive rate (TPR) against the false positive rate (FPR) at various threshold values.

- **True Positive Rate (TPR)**: Sensitivity or Recall.
- **False Positive Rate (FPR)**: The proportion of actual negatives incorrectly classified as positive.

The area under the curve (AUC) gives a measure of how well the model can distinguish between the two classes. A higher AUC indicates better model performance, with a perfect model achieving an AUC of 1.

5.4.3   Intersection over Union (IoU)

Intersection over Union (IoU) is commonly used in object detection and segmentation tasks, especially when dealing with geospatial imagery. It measures the overlap between the predicted and true objects of interest (e.g., land cover types, buildings, water bodies).

$$IoU = \frac{Area_{Intersection}}{Area_{Union}}$$

Where: - **Area of Intersection** is the area covered by both the predicted and true objects. - **Area of Union** is the total area covered by either the predicted or true objects.

IoU values range from 0 to 1, where a higher value indicates better accuracy. In object detection tasks, an IoU threshold (e.g., 0.5) is often used to determine whether a prediction is considered correct.

5.4.4   Confusion Matrix

A confusion matrix is a table used to evaluate the performance of a classification model, providing a breakdown of correct and incorrect classifications. It shows how many instances were classified correctly versus incorrectly for each class. This matrix is particularly helpful for understanding the types of errors made by a model.

	$Predicted\ Positive$	$Predicted\ Negative$
$Actual\ Positive$	$TruePositive(TP)$	$FalseNegative(FN)$
$Actual\ Negative$	$FalsePositive(FP)$	$TrueNegative(TN)$

5.4.5   Overall Accuracy

Overall accuracy is simply the proportion of correctly classified instances out of all instances. However, it may not be a reliable metric in cases of class imbalance, where one class is dominant.

$$Accuracy = \frac{TP + TN}{TP + TN + FP + FN}$$

Although this metric is simple and intuitive, it should be used with caution when classes are imbalanced.

5.5 Challenges in Model Validation

5.5.1 Overfitting

Overfitting occurs when a model learns the noise in the training data instead of the underlying patterns. This leads to a poor generalization on new and unseen data. To detect overfitting, it is crucial to compare the model's performance on training and validation datasets. If the model performs well on the training data but poorly on the validation data, overfitting is likely.

5.5.2 Data Imbalance

In geospatial deep learning tasks, class imbalance (e.g., more examples of urban areas than forests in land cover classification) is common. Traditional metrics such as overall accuracy may be misleading in such cases. Therefore, metrics such as F1 score, AUC-ROC, and IoU are often more informative.

5.6 Best Practices for Model Validation and Accuracy Assessment

To ensure robust model performance in geospatial deep learning tasks, consider the following best practices:

- **Use Spatial k-Fold Cross-Validation** to account for spatial autocorrelation in geospatial datasets.
- **Complement Accuracy with Other Metrics**: Use the F1 score, AUC-ROC, and IoU for a more informative model evaluation, especially in imbalanced datasets.
- **Visualize Performance**: Visualizing confusion matrices, ROC curves, and prediction maps can provide valuable insight into the behavior of the model.
- **Use a Test Set**: After model selection, always test the final model on a separate test set to assess real-world performance.

- **Regularize the Model**: To avoid overfitting, apply techniques such as dropout, weight decay, and data augmentation.

5.7 Summary

- Model validation and accuracy assessment are critical to ensuring the effectiveness of geospatial deep learning models.
- Spatial k-fold cross-validation addresses spatial dependence issues in geospatial data and is essential for realistic performance estimates.
- Metrics like the F1-score, AUC-ROC, and IoU provide a comprehensive view of model performance, especially in imbalanced datasets or segmentation tasks.
- Overfitting is a common challenge, and it can be mitigated by using proper validation techniques and regularization methods.

Exercise Questions

(1) Explain the difference between traditional k-fold cross-validation and spatial k-fold cross-validation. Why is the latter preferred in geospatial tasks?
(2) Describe how the F1-score is calculated and why it is particularly useful in imbalanced datasets.
(3) What is the AUC-ROC curve, and how would you interpret its results?
(4) Discuss the potential drawbacks of using overall accuracy as the sole metric for model evaluation.

Notes and Suggestions

- Always validate your model using multiple metrics to get a more complete picture of its performance.
- Practice evaluating models on different geospatial datasets to understand how different regions and patterns affect model performance.
- Explore advanced model validation techniques, such as stratified k-fold cross-validation and bootstrapping.

Chapter 6

Reproducibility and Open Science in Spatial AI

Learning Objectives

At the end of this chapter, you should be able to:

- Understand the importance of reproducibility in geospatial artificial intelligence (Spatial AI).
- Learn about open science and its significance for collaboration and progress in Spatial AI.
- Explore best practices for sharing data, code, and models in Spatial AI projects.
- Understand how to use platforms such as GitHub, Zenodo, and Google Earth Engine for sharing and disseminating research.
- Appreciate the role of version control and documentation in ensuring reproducibility.

6.1 Introduction

Reproducibility is one of the cornerstones of scientific research, ensuring that experiments and models can be reliably replicated, validated, and extended by other researchers. In the realm of geospatial artificial intelligence (Spatial AI), reproducibility is especially important, given the complexity of geospatial data and the multidisciplinary nature of the field. Open science practices, which advocate for the open sharing of data, code, and results, have become essential to foster collaboration, improve transparency, and accelerate innovation.

This chapter discusses the principles of reproducibility and open science in the context of Spatial AI. It covers best practices for publishing and sharing data and code using popular platforms such as GitHub, Zenodo, and Google Earth Engine. Following these practices enhances collaboration, ensures research integrity, and helps researchers and practitioners in the geospatial domain replicate and build upon existing work.

6.2   The Importance of Reproducibility in Spatial AI

Reproducibility refers to the ability to replicate the results of a study or experiment using the same data, methods, and analysis. In the context of Spatial AI, reproducibility allows researchers to confirm the reliability of geospatial models, ensure consistency across different geographical areas, and prevent erroneous conclusions that may arise from biased or incomplete datasets.

The spatial nature of the data involved in geospatial AI, such as satellite imagery, geographical features, and environmental data, adds a layer of complexity to reproducibility. A model trained on one set of geographic data may not perform well in another region due to differences in terrain, climate, or spatial distribution. Therefore, open sharing of geospatial data, models, and results is critical for others to assess and validate findings, as well as for improving the generalization of models across diverse spatial contexts.

6.3   Open Science and Collaboration in Spatial AI

Open science is the practice of making scientific research, data, and knowledge freely accessible to others, enabling greater collaboration, transparency, and innovation. In the field of Spatial AI, open science can take several forms:

- **Open Data**: Sharing raw datasets, such as satellite imagery, land-use/land-cover data, or environmental monitoring data.
- **Open Code**: Sharing the source code for data processing, model training, and analysis pipelines, often through version control systems like Git.
- **Open Models**: Sharing pre-trained machine learning models, which can be reused or fine-tuned for similar tasks.
- **Open Results**: Publishing analysis results and performance metrics, often accompanied by reproducible workflows.

By embracing open science principles, researchers in Spatial AI can build upon each other's work, avoid redundant research efforts, and accelerate the development of more robust and generalizable models.

6.4 Best Practices for Publishing Data, Code, and Models

6.4.1 Using GitHub for Version Control and Collaboration

GitHub is one of the most widely used platforms for sharing and collaborating on code. It allows researchers to store, track, and manage their code repositories in a version-controlled environment. Here are some best practices for using GitHub in Spatial AI research:

- **Repository Structure**: Organize your repository in a clear and logical manner. A typical Spatial AI repository might include directories for raw data (e.g., satellite imagery), code (e.g., model training scripts), results (e.g., performance metrics), and documentation (e.g., readme files).
- **Documentation**: Ensure that your repository is well-documented. Include a detailed README file that explains the purpose of the project, how to run the code, the dependencies required, and any other relevant information.
- **License**: Choose an appropriate license for your code (e.g., MIT, GPL) to clarify how others can use and contribute to your work. This is particularly important in open science.
- **Issues and Pull Requests**: Use GitHub's issue tracker to keep track of bugs, enhancements, and discussions. Pull requests (PRs) are useful for collaborating on changes to the codebase and reviewing contributions from others.
- **Branching**: Use branching to manage different stages of development (e.g., experimentation, testing, production). This keeps the main codebase clean and allows for experimentation without affecting the stability of the project.

6.4.2 Zenodo for Data and Model Archiving

Zenodo is an open-access repository for research data, which is integrated with GitHub to make it easier for researchers to archive and share their datasets and models. Zenodo issues a DOI (Digital Object Identifier) for each upload, making it easier to cite datasets and models in academic papers.

- **Archiving Data and Models**: When your Spatial AI research involves large datasets or pre-trained models, Zenodo is an excellent platform for making them publicly available.

Ensure that datasets are well-organized and include metadata (e.g., dataset description, creator, publication date).

- **Citing Zenodo**: When publishing research papers, you can cite datasets and models hosted on Zenodo using the DOI, which provides a permanent link to the resource.
- **Versioning**: Zenodo supports versioning, so you can upload new versions of your datasets or models. This ensures that others can access the most up-to-date version of your work.

6.4.3 Google Earth Engine Apps for Sharing Geospatial Analysis

Google Earth Engine (GEE) is a powerful cloud-based platform for geospatial analysis, particularly for working with satellite imagery and large geospatial datasets. Earth Engine Apps allows you to create interactive web applications that showcase your geospatial analysis results.

- **Sharing Earth Engine Apps**: After developing a geospatial analysis pipeline or model in GEE, you can share your work with the broader community by creating Earth Engine Apps. These apps can be used to visualize and interact with geospatial data, model outputs, and analysis results in an intuitive way.
- **Collaboration**: Earth Engine allows collaboration by sharing your scripts or apps with other researchers, making it easier to work together on geospatial AI projects.
- **Reproducible Workflows**: By sharing your Earth Engine scripts publicly, others can replicate your geospatial analysis and apply it to different datasets or regions.

6.5 Publishing Results with Interactive Maps

One of the key aspects of ensuring reproducibility and open science is making research results easily accessible and understandable. For geospatial data, this often means creating **interactive maps** that allow users to explore the data dynamically. Two commonly used tools for publishing interactive maps are **Leaflet** and **Dash**.

6.5.1 Leaflet

Leaflet is a popular JavaScript library for creating interactive maps that can be embedded in web pages. It's lightweight, easy to use, and highly customizable. Researchers and practitioners can use Leaflet to create map-based visualizations of geospatial data, enabling users to interact with maps and explore different layers, zoom in on specific areas, and gain deeper insights into spatial patterns.

Use case: A common example in Spatial AI is visualizing satellite imagery or model predictions (e.g., land use/land cover changes) on a map. Researchers can publish these maps online and share links with collaborators or the public.

Best Practices for Leaflet:

- Use clear and consistent legends to explain different map layers.
- Ensure the map is interactive and can handle zooming and panning smoothly.
- Include metadata with the map to explain the data sources, processing steps, and limitations.

6.5.2 Dash by Plotly

Dash is a Python framework for building web applications with interactive visualizations. It is particularly suited for data science and machine learning applications, including geospatial analysis. Dash allows you to create dashboards that integrate maps, charts, and other visualizations in an interactive and user-friendly way. Dash also supports callbacks, enabling dynamic updates to the visualizations based on user input.

Use case: Researchers can use Dash to create web apps that allow users to interact with geospatial models, such as selecting different spatial features or toggling between model outputs (e.g., land cover predictions, climate projections).

Best Practices for Dash:

- Combine multiple types of visualizations (e.g., maps, plots, tables) for a comprehensive view of the data.
- Ensure the application is responsive and works across devices (desktop, tablet, mobile).
- Optimize performance by reducing the data size or complexity, especially for large-scale geospatial datasets.

6.5.3 Example Workflow for Interactive Map Publishing

(1) **Data Preparation**: Process and analyze geospatial data using Python or GIS tools.
(2) **Interactive Map Creation**: Use Leaflet or Dash to create interactive maps.
(3) **Web Hosting**: Host the map on a public or private server to share with others.
(4) **Documentation**: Provide clear explanations and metadata to ensure others can understand and reproduce the work.

6.6 Version Control and Documentation for Reproducibility

6.6.1 Importance of Version Control

Version control systems, such as Git, play a vital role in ensuring reproducibility in Spatial AI research. By tracking changes to code and data, version control allows you to go back to previous versions of your work, collaborate with others, and ensure that your analysis is consistent across different stages of development.

- **Git**: Use Git to track changes to your codebase and dataset. With Git, you can maintain a history of changes and manage contributions from multiple collaborators.
- **GitHub Actions**: GitHub Actions can be used to automate workflows, such as running tests on your code or automatically deploying your analysis to cloud platforms. This helps maintain a high level of quality control.

6.6.2 Documentation Practices

Clear and thorough documentation is essential for reproducibility. Ensure that your project includes the following:

- **README File**: Provide a summary of the project, installation instructions, how to run the code, and any required dependencies.
- **Jupyter Notebooks**: For geospatial AI tasks, Jupyter notebooks are excellent for documenting your analysis while keeping code and results together in an interactive environment.
- **Metadata**: Include metadata with your datasets to describe their structure, content, and any processing steps that have been applied. This is especially important when sharing satellite imagery or other large geospatial datasets.

6.7 Challenges and Solutions

6.7.1 Data Privacy and Licensing

One challenge in open science is ensuring that sensitive data is not inadvertently shared. In geospatial AI, some datasets, particularly those involving personal information or national security, cannot be shared publicly.

- **Data Anonymization**: Ensure that any personal or sensitive information in your datasets is anonymized before publication.

- **License Restrictions**: Make sure that the datasets you share are properly licensed. Use open licenses (e.g., Creative Commons) when possible, but be aware of any restrictions imposed by data providers.

6.7.2 Ensuring Model Reproducibility

In geospatial AI, models often rely on complex pipelines and large datasets. Ensuring that others can reproduce your model's results can be challenging, especially when models require significant computational resources.

- **Containerization**: Use Docker or similar containerization technologies to create reproducible environments for model training and inference. This ensures that your code and dependencies are packaged together, making it easier for others to reproduce your work.
- **Cloud Platforms**: For computationally intensive models, consider using cloud platforms like Google Cloud, AWS, or Microsoft Azure to provide access to the necessary resources.

6.8 Summary

In this chapter, we have discussed the importance of reproducibility and open science in Spatial AI. We explored best practices for publishing data, code, and models using platforms such as GitHub, Zenodo, and Earth Engine. Embracing open science practices enhances collaboration, ensures transparency, and accelerates the development of geospatial AI technologies. By following these best practices, researchers can ensure that their work is reproducible, reliable, and accessible to the wider scientific community.

Exercise Questions

(1) What is the importance of reproducibility in Spatial AI? How does it impact the reliability of geospatial models?

(2) Explain the concept of open science. Why is it crucial in the context of Spatial AI research?

(3) What are the best practices for publishing data and code in Spatial AI research? Mention the platforms commonly used for this purpose.

(4) How can version control systems like GitHub contribute to the reproducibility of Spatial AI projects?

(5) Describe how Zenodo can be used to share research outputs. What are the advantages of using Zenodo for academic research?

(6) What is the role of Google Earth Engine in ensuring reproducibility for geospatial research? Provide examples of its application.

(7) What are some common challenges researchers face when implementing reproducibility in Spatial AI? How can these challenges be overcome?

Notes and Suggestions

- Tip for Publishing Data: Always ensure that your datasets are well-documented. Include metadata that describes the data's source, date of collection, preprocessing steps, and any transformations applied.

- Pro Tip for Code Sharing: When sharing code on platforms like GitHub, provide clear documentation and comments. This will help other researchers understand the structure of the code and how to use it effectively.

- Pro Tip for Zenodo: When uploading research outputs to Zenodo, make sure to use relevant keywords and tags to make your work discoverable. Zenodo provides DOIs (Digital Object Identifiers), which enhance the citation and credibility of your work.

- Best Practice for Version Control: Use GitHub to store your project code. Create meaningful commit messages that describe the changes made at each step. This helps ensure that others can trace the evolution of your project and replicate your results.

- Recommendation for Collaboration: Collaborate with other researchers through open repositories like GitHub or GitLab. Regularly update your codebase, and encourage others to contribute, ensuring that your work evolves with new insights.

- Common Challenge: A major challenge in geospatial AI is ensuring the availability of high-quality, region-specific datasets. Consider seeking partnerships with governmental or non-profit organizations that specialize in geospatial data collection and distribution.

- Recommended Tools: For geospatial AI research, using a combination of open tools such as Google Earth Engine and QGIS along with cloud computing platforms like AWS or Google Cloud can streamline the process of data analysis and model deployment.

Part III

Applications and Case Studies

Chapter **7**

Mapping Mangrove Ecosystems Using Deep Learning: A Case Study from Coastal Maharashtra

Learning Objectives

At the end of this chapter, you should be able to:

- Explain the significance and mapping challenges of mangroves using remote sensing.
- Apply CNNs to classify natural habitats from satellite data.
- Describe the deep learning pipeline for geospatial data.
- Compare CNNs with traditional machine learning methods for land cover classification.
- Evaluate model accuracy and classification maps.
- Understand the limitations and potential of deep learning in environmental monitoring.

7.1 Introduction

Mangroves are specialized coastal forests that thrive in saline and brackish waters along tropical and subtropical coastlines. They play a crucial role in maintaining ecological balance by stabilizing shorelines, reducing coastal erosion, providing breeding grounds for marine biodiversity, and acting as significant carbon sinks. Despite their importance, mangrove ecosystems are increasingly threatened by anthropogenic activities such as deforestation, aquaculture, and urban development, as well as by climate-induced factors like sea-level rise and changes in tidal patterns.

Mapping and monitoring mangrove forests are vital for sustainable coastal resource management and climate resilience planning. Traditional field-based mapping is accurate but limited by logistical, temporal, and cost constraints. Remote sensing technologies, particularly with the availability of high-resolution satellite imagery, have enabled broader and more frequent assessment of mangrove cover.

In recent years, deep learning has emerged as a transformative technology in geospatial analysis. Its ability to automatically learn complex patterns from data has made it particularly suited for applications involving image classification, such as land cover mapping. This chapter explores the use of Convolutional Neural Networks (CNNs) for the classification of mangrove and non-mangrove areas from multispectral satellite imagery, leveraging a case study from the coastal districts of Maharashtra, India.

Note: *The study presented in this chapter is adapted from the author's doctoral dissertation, which investigated deep learning techniques for geospatial data analysis, focusing on ecosystem mapping, including mangrove forest classification.*

7.2   Ecological Importance of Mangrove Ecosystems

Mangroves are considered one of the most productive and ecologically significant ecosystems on Earth. They provide numerous ecosystem services that benefit both the environment and coastal communities. Key roles include:

- **Biodiversity Hotspots:** Mangroves support a wide range of terrestrial and marine species, serving as nurseries for fish, crustaceans, and mollusks.
- **Carbon Sequestration:** Mangrove forests store substantial amounts of carbon in both biomass and soil, contributing to climate mitigation.
- **Coastal Defense:** Their dense root systems reduce wave energy, protect against storm surges, and prevent shoreline erosion.
- **Livelihood Support:** Many coastal communities depend on mangroves for fuel, timber, and non-timber forest products.

Despite their resilience to salinity and flooding, mangroves are highly sensitive to changes in land use and water regimes. Remote sensing offers a powerful tool to regularly assess mangrove health and coverage, particularly when combined with advanced image analysis techniques such as deep learning.

7.3 Study Area: Coastal Districts of Maharashtra

The study was conducted across five major coastal districts of Maharashtra: Mumbai City, Mumbai Suburb, Raigad, Ratnagiri, and Sindhudurg. These districts lie along the Arabian Sea and are characterized by diverse topography including estuaries, tidal creeks, and deltas—conditions favorable for mangrove growth.

- **Mumbai Region:** Highly urbanized, with fragmented mangrove patches amid industrial and residential development.
- **Raigad and Ratnagiri:** Coastal plains with significant agricultural and aquaculture activity.
- **Sindhudurg:** Known for relatively undisturbed and dense mangrove belts, making it ideal for training a classification model.

These districts collectively host one of the largest mangrove stretches on the western coast of India. However, land-use changes have accelerated the need for regular monitoring using satellite-based and AI-driven tools.

7.4 Data Acquisition and Satellite Imagery Specifications

In this study, imagery from the Landsat 8 Operational Land Imager (OLI) was used to classify mangrove and non-mangrove areas. Landsat 8 was selected for its balance of spatial resolution, spectral richness, and open access availability, making it a practical choice for large-area vegetation studies.

Satellite Platform: Landsat 8

Landsat 8 provides multispectral data with a spatial resolution of 30 meters (for most bands) and a revisit frequency of 16 days. The sensor captures 11 spectral bands, of which three were used in this study:

- **Band 4 (Red):** 0.63–0.68 µm – useful for detecting chlorophyll absorption in vegetation.
- **Band 5 (NIR):** 0.85–0.88 µm – critical for vegetation biomass and moisture content.

- **Band 6 (SWIR 1):** 1.57–1.65 µm – helps differentiate vegetation from soil and detect water stress.

The data was obtained from the USGS Earth Explorer platform, ensuring high-quality and cloud-free scenes aligned with the seasonal vegetation cycle (post-monsoon period, November–January).

Ground Truth and Label Generation

To create reliable training data, ground truth points for mangrove and non-mangrove areas were generated using:

- Field knowledge and previous surveys.
- Visual interpretation using high-resolution Google Earth imagery.
- Existing LULC maps from the Maharashtra Remote Sensing Application Centre (MR-SAC).

These labeled samples were subsequently used to train and validate the classification models.

7.5 Image Preprocessing and Tile Generation

Satellite imagery must undergo preprocessing to prepare it for deep learning tasks. Pre-processing ensures consistency in the input data and allows the model to focus on learning relevant spatial and spectral patterns.

Steps in Preprocessing:

(1) **Band Stacking:** The selected bands (Red, NIR, and SWIR) were combined into a single multiband raster to capture vegetation characteristics.

(2) **Radiometric Correction:** Raw pixel values (digital numbers) were converted to top-of-atmosphere reflectance to normalize lighting differences across scenes.

(3) **Clipping:** The composite image was clipped to the boundaries of the study districts using a shapefile in ArcGIS Pro.

(4) **Normalization:** Each band was normalized using min-max scaling, transforming pixel values to a [0,1] range for numerical stability during training.

(5) **Tiling:** The full image was divided into 256×256 pixel tiles. This size was chosen to balance contextual information and computational efficiency.

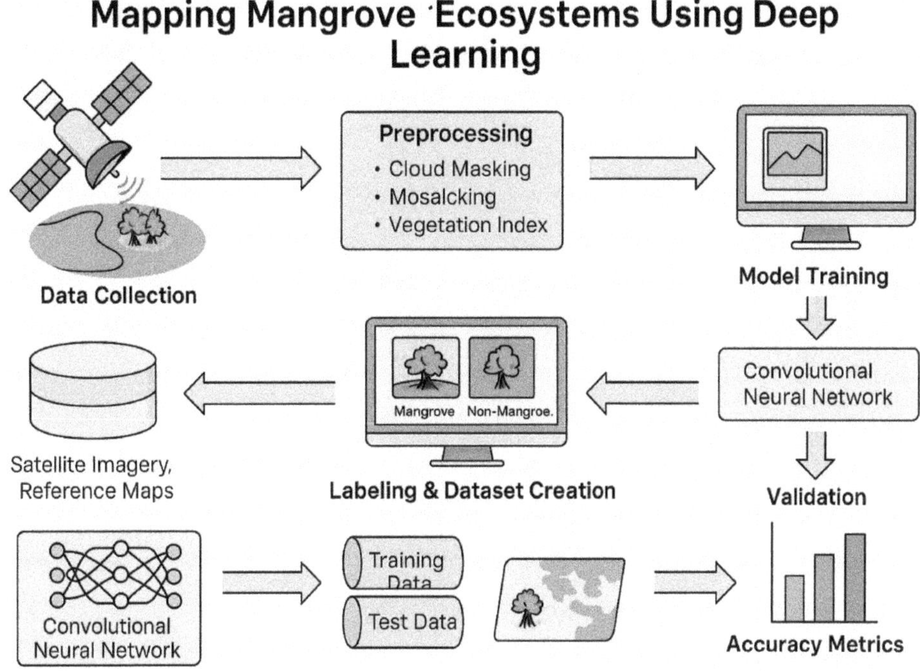

Figure 7.1: Workflow for Mapping Mangroves using Deep Learning

Data Augmentation

To overcome the limited number of labeled tiles and improve the generalization ability of the CNN, data augmentation was applied:

- **Rotations:** 90°, 180°, and 270°.
- **Horizontal and Vertical Flips.**
- **Zoom and Cropping:** To simulate different viewing scales.

This increased the mangrove classification dataset from 556 raw tiles to over 904 image tiles, ensuring a more balanced and diverse set of inputs for the model.

7.6   CNN Architecture for Mangrove Classification

Convolutional Neural Networks (CNNs) are especially effective at learning spatial patterns in imagery. Unlike traditional classifiers that rely on manually engineered features, CNNs learn filters directly from data during training. This enables the automatic detection of subtle spectral and spatial characteristics unique to mangrove regions.

Model Design Overview

The architecture designed for this study was built using TensorFlow and Keras on Google Colab, allowing free GPU support. The CNN consisted of multiple convolutional and pooling layers, culminating in a dense classification layer.

- **Input:** A 256×256 grayscale tile derived from multispectral bands.
- **Conv Layer 1:** 32 filters of size 3×3 with ReLU activation.
- **Max Pooling:** Downsampling by a factor of 2×2.
- **Conv Layer 2:** 64 filters with ReLU + Max Pooling.
- **Conv Layer 3:** 128 filters + ReLU + Max Pooling.
- **Conv Layer 4:** 256 filters + ReLU + Max Pooling.
- **Flatten Layer:** Converts feature maps into a 1D vector.
- **Dense Layer:** 256 neurons with ReLU activation.
- **Dropout:** Applied at 0.25 to prevent overfitting.
- **Output Layer:** Sigmoid activation for binary classification (mangrove vs. non-mangrove).

This model was trained using binary cross-entropy loss, with an Adam optimizer and batch size of 32 over 50 epochs.

7.7 Model Training and Performance Evaluation

7.7.1 Training Procedure

The CNN model was trained on Google Colab with GPU acceleration. The total training time was approximately 20 minutes for 50 epochs. The binary cross-entropy loss function was minimized using the Adam optimizer, which adaptively adjusts the learning rate during training.

7.7.2 Monitoring Training Progress

To track training progress and detect overfitting, both training and validation accuracy and loss were plotted using Matplotlib and TensorBoard callbacks. Early stopping was enabled to halt training if the validation loss did not improve after five consecutive epochs.

7.7.3 Evaluation Metrics

Post-training, the model was evaluated using the following metrics:

- **Accuracy** The overall correctness of the classification is given by:

Table 7.1: CNN Model Performance on Mangrove Classification

Metric	Value
Accuracy	84.926%
Precision	100%
Recall	84.92%
F1 Score	91.84%

$$\text{Accuracy} = \frac{TP + TN}{TP + TN + FP + FN}$$

where:

- TP = True Positive (correctly predicted positive cases)
- TN = True Negative (correctly predicted negative cases)
- FP = False Positive (incorrectly predicted as positive)
- FN = False Negative (incorrectly predicted as negative)

- **Precision:** Correct positive predictions out of total positive predictions.

$$\text{Precision} = \frac{TP}{TP + FP}$$

- **Recall (Sensitivity):** Correct positive predictions out of actual positives.

$$\text{Recall} = \frac{TP}{TP + FN}$$

- **F1 Score:** Harmonic mean of precision and recall.

$$\text{F1 Score} = 2 \times \frac{\text{Precision} \times \text{Recall}}{\text{Precision} + \text{Recall}}$$

- **Confusion Matrix:** Tabulates predicted vs. actual classes, with the following structure:

$$\begin{bmatrix} TP & FP \\ FN & TN \end{bmatrix}$$

7.8   Comparison with Random Forest Classifier

To benchmark the performance of the CNN, a Random Forest (RF) classifier was also trained using the same dataset. RF is a widely-used ensemble learning technique based on decision trees and often serves as a baseline in geospatial classification tasks.

Table 7.2: Random Forest Model Performance

Metric	Value
Accuracy	76.47%
Precision	76.5%
Recall	76.5%
F1 Score	76%

Results

The RF classifier achieved an accuracy of 76.47% with a lower precision and F1 scores than CNN. Although the RF model is easier to interpret and faster to train, it lacked the spatial pattern learning capabilities that CNNs excel at.

Thus the CNN model produced smoother classification boundaries and better detected continuous mangrove patches, while RF produced more fragmented results.

7.9   Summary

This chapter demonstrated the application of Convolutional Neural Networks for mapping mangrove ecosystems using multispectral Landsat-8 data. The study, derived from the author's doctoral research, showcased a real-world geospatial deep learning pipeline—from satellite image preparation and preprocessing, to CNN model development and evaluation.

The CNN model achieved over 84.926% classification accuracy and outperformed a Random Forest classifier in precision, recall, and spatial coherence. This highlights CNN's ability to learn contextual and spectral features in remotely sensed imagery. The findings reinforce the value of deep learning for ecological monitoring and suggest its potential for scalable deployment across other coastal zones.

Exercise Questions

(1) Why are mangrove ecosystems critical for coastal resilience and biodiversity?

(2) List the main spectral bands used from Landsat-8 in this case study and justify their selection.

(3) Describe the image preprocessing steps and explain the rationale behind data tiling and augmentation.

(4) Explain the CNN architecture used in this study. What roles do convolution and pooling layers play?

(5) Compare the performance and output of CNN and Random Forest models based on

this case study.

(6) Identify the challenges in training deep learning models for environmental data like mangroves.

Notes and Suggestions

- Students are encouraged to replicate this case study using openly available Landsat data and Google Colab.
- Explore tools such as `Rasterio`, `EarthPy`, and `torchgeo` for spatial data handling in Python.
- Consider experimenting with U-Net architecture for improved pixel-level segmentation.
- For further reading, explore case studies published in journals such as *Remote Sensing of Environment* and *IEEE JSTARS*.
- Extend this study to time-series analysis by combining CNNs with RNNs or using multi-temporal classification frameworks.

Chapter 8

LULC Change Detection Using Machine Learning

Learning Objectives

At the end of this chapter, you should be able to:

- Understand the concept and significance of Land Use and Land Cover (LULC) change detection.
- Explore the application of machine learning techniques for remote sensing data classification.
- Learn how Random Forest classifiers can be used for LULC mapping using Landsat imagery.
- Analyze the spatial and temporal changes in Raigad district's land cover from 2002 to 2021.
- Assess the strengths and limitations of classical ML methods for geospatial analysis.

8.1 Introduction

Land Use and Land Cover (LULC) change detection is a crucial component of geospatial analysis and environmental monitoring. It allows researchers and policymakers to understand the extent and nature of transformations in the landscape over time. These changes can be driven by both anthropogenic activities such as urban expansion and natural processes like deforestation, making LULC change detection essential for sustainable planning and conservation efforts.

In this chapter, we present a machine learning-based approach for LULC change detection, grounded in the work carried out in the Raigad district of Maharashtra, India, as part of our thesis research. The study utilizes Landsat satellite imagery over a period of 20 years (2002–2021) and evaluates Random Forest classifiers for LULC classification and change detection.

8.2   Motivation and Research Objectives

Raigad, a coastal district of Maharashtra known for its ecological richness and tourism potential, has undergone significant land cover changes in the last two decades. Infrastructure developments, particularly road network expansions, have contributed to deforestation and vegetation loss.

This study aims to:

(1) Map the LULC of Raigad district for the years 2002 and 2021.
(2) Detect and quantify the changes in land cover over the 20-year period.
(3) Apply Random Forest classifiers for LULC classification using region-specific satellite imagery.
(4) Evaluate the performance of the chosen method using appropriate accuracy metrics.

8.3   Dataset Description

8.3.1   Landsat Imagery for Raigad

Landsat 7 and Landsat 8 imagery were used to generate high-resolution, cloud-free composite images for Raigad district over the 2002–2021 timeframe. Imagery preprocessing involved filtering for cloud cover, radiometric corrections, and band selection in the visible, NIR, and SWIR ranges.

8.4   Methodology

This section describes the methodology followed for mapping and analyzing land use and land cover (LULC) changes using Landsat satellite imagery and machine learning techniques. The workflow was designed to ensure systematic data acquisition, preprocessing, classification, and result visualization, as illustrated in Figure 10.1.

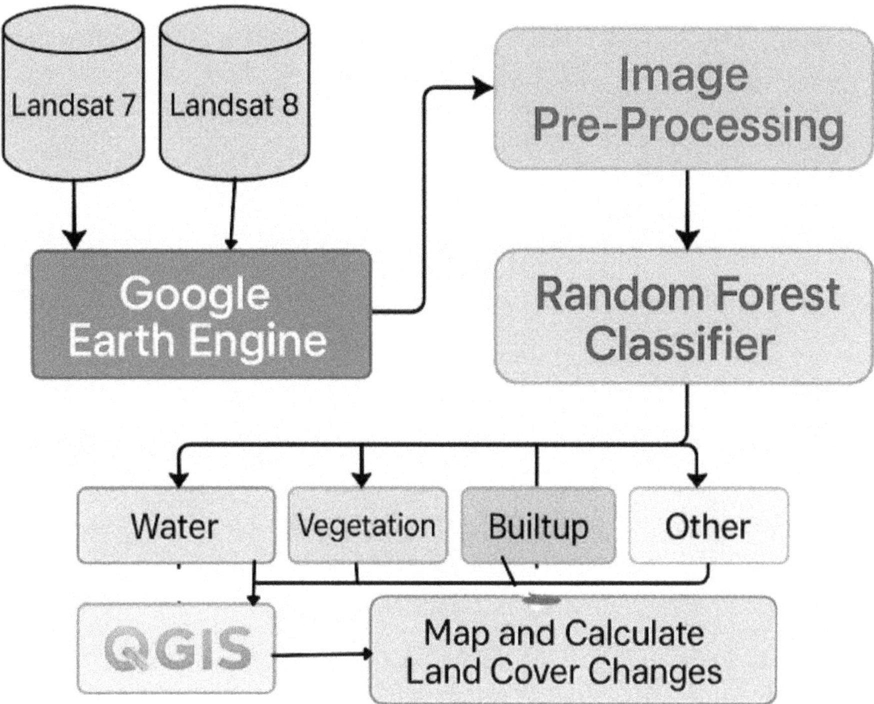

Figure 8.1: Workflow for Land Use Land Cover (LULC) classification and change detection.

8.4.1 Data Acquisition

Satellite imagery from **Landsat 7** and **Landsat 8** was utilized for this study. These datasets provide multispectral images with moderate spatial resolution, suitable for regional-scale land cover classification. The images were sourced via the Google Earth Engine (GEE) platform, which offers cloud-based access to a wide archive of remotely sensed data.

8.4.2 Data Import and Preparation

The acquired Landsat images were imported into the Google Earth Engine environment. The study area boundary was defined using a vector shapefile representing the region of interest. Each image was **clipped** to this boundary to limit the analysis to the specified region.

8.4.3 Image Pre-Processing

To ensure the quality and consistency of input data, the following preprocessing steps were performed:

- **Filtering:** Images were filtered based on the required time period for analysis.
- **Spectral Band Selection:** Specific spectral bands relevant for land cover classification were selected.
- **Mosaic Creation:** Cloud-free mosaics were generated for each year by compositing multiple images, minimizing the impact of cloud cover and other artifacts.

8.4.4 Image Classification

A **Random Forest Classifier**, a supervised machine learning algorithm, was employed for classifying the preprocessed imagery. Training datasets representing various land cover classes — such as *Water*, *Vegetation*, *Built-up*, and *Other* — were prepared using high-resolution reference data and expert interpretation. The classifier was trained on these samples and applied to classify the entire mosaicked images.

8.4.5 Post-Processing and Analysis

The classified maps were then post-processed to correct minor classification errors. The final classified outputs were used to:

- **Map land cover categories.**
- **Quantify land cover changes** over the study period.

8.4.6 Result Export and Visualization

The classified LULC maps were exported from Google Earth Engine and imported into **QGIS** for detailed visualization and further spatial analysis. QGIS facilitated the creation of thematic maps and the calculation of area statistics for each land cover category.

8.5 Results and Discussion

8.5.1 LULC Change Detection in Raigad

The comprehensive LULC mapping analysis of Raigad district, spanning the period from 2002 to 2021, has shed light on the dynamic transformations within the coastal region of Maharashtra, India. The study harnessed the power of Google Earth Engine (GEE) to

Table 8.1: Random Forest Model Performance on LULC Mapping

Model	Accuracy	Precision	Recall	F1 Score
Random Forest	84.49 %	90.04 %	89.68 %	89.84 %

assess and document changes in land cover, encompassing four primary categories: Water, Vegetation, Built-up, and Other.

Key takeaways from the investigation include:

(1) **Temporal Evolution of Land Cover:** This analysis revealed significant temporal variations in land cover classes, with notable trends including urban expansion, increased built-up areas, and alterations in vegetation cover. These changes underscore the evolving nature of Raigad's landscape, which has implications for both its aesthetic appeal and ecological balance.

(2) **Spatial Patterns:** Spatially, distinct patterns were observed in land cover distributions across Raigad district. These patterns are influenced by factors such as topography, proximity to coastal regions, and urban development. The thematic maps vividly depict these spatial variations, providing valuable insights for regional planning and management.

(3) **Change Detection:** The assessment of land cover change showcased areas of concern, particularly where the district's natural beauty and ecosystems have experienced significant alterations. Notable findings include vegetation loss due to road widening projects and shifts in water bodies, both of which demand attention in terms of environmental conservation and sustainable development.

(4) **Accuracy and Validation:** The LULC classification was rigorously validated, ensuring the reliability of the results. The use of robust performance metrics and validation methods strengthened the accuracy of the classification model.

(5) **Future Directions:** It is imperative to acknowledge that land cover dynamics are ongoing. Future research should focus on continuous monitoring and prediction to support informed decision-making for the region's sustainable development, tourism management, and environmental preservation.

8.5.2 Classification Performance

The Random Forest classifier demonstrated robust performance on region-specific LULC classification, validating its effectiveness in scenarios with moderate computational resources and labeled data availability.

8.6 Conclusion

This study demonstrates the utility of classical machine learning approaches, such as Random Forest, for LULC change detection. By leveraging cloud-based platforms like Google Earth Engine for preprocessing and region-specific analysis, the framework offers a scalable and effective solution for long-term land monitoring.

The Raigad case study underscores the critical importance of continuous LULC monitoring in ecologically sensitive and rapidly transforming regions. Given Raigad's unique blend of biodiversity, coastal ecosystems, and increasing anthropogenic pressure from urbanization and tourism, timely detection of land cover changes is vital. The findings highlight the urgency of implementing robust conservation strategies and data-driven policy planning to safeguard the region's environmental integrity and ensure sustainable development.

8.7 Future Work

Future efforts may include:

- Integrating temporal machine learning models for better time-series prediction.
- Exploring deep learning architectures tailored specifically to LULC problems in Indian geographic contexts.
- Incorporating socio-economic and climate variables for multi-criteria LULC analysis.

Summary

This chapter explored the application of machine learning for LULC change detection in Raigad district over a 20-year period. Using Landsat data and Random Forest classification within Google Earth Engine, we successfully mapped spatial and temporal land cover changes. The approach yielded an 84.49% accuracy and identified key trends like urban expansion and vegetation loss. This methodology provides a scalable template for other regional LULC studies.

Exercise Questions

(1) Explain the significance of LULC change detection in environmental planning.
(2) Describe the process of preprocessing Landsat imagery for classification.
(3) Discuss the merits and demerits of using Random Forest for LULC classification.
(4) How does Google Earth Engine facilitate large-scale remote sensing analysis?

(5) Suggest improvements or extensions to this study.

Notes and Suggestions

- Consider incorporating NDVI or other vegetation indices to enhance classification performance.
- Visualization of change maps can improve interpretability; include them in your future reports.
- Future work may benefit from ensemble learning approaches or neural network-based classifiers.
- Cross-validate with ground truth data or high-resolution imagery where feasible.

Chapter 9

Landslide Susceptibility Prediction Using Machine Learning – A Case Study from Raigad District

Learning Objectives

At the end of this chapter, you should be able to:

- Understand the importance of landslide susceptibility prediction as a geospatial task.
- Learn how geospatial conditioning factors influence landslide occurrence.
- Explore the use of Multi-Layer Perceptron (MLP) models for multi-class classification.
- Analyze real-world landslide data from Raigad district and apply geospatial preprocessing.
- Evaluate machine learning models using classification performance metrics.

9.1   Introduction

Landslides are sudden, fast-moving events where a mass of earth or rock moves down a slope. They are triggered by various factors such as intense rainfall, earthquakes, human activities, and changes in land use patterns. These events pose serious threats to life, property, infrastructure, and the environment. Raigad district in the Konkan region of Maharashtra is particularly prone to landslides due to its rugged topography, heavy monsoon precipitation, and deforestation caused by urbanization and infrastructure development.

The prediction and mapping of landslide-prone areas can help in disaster preparedness and sustainable land-use planning. This chapter introduces an approach rooted in geospatial analysis and machine learning, specifically using a Multi-Layer Perceptron (MLP), to model and predict landslide susceptibility in Raigad. The study draws upon the author's Ph.D. research and offers a comprehensive case study for students and practitioners interested in integrating GIS, remote sensing, and AI tools for hazard assessment.

9.2 Significance of Landslide Prediction as a Geospatial Task

Landslide prediction requires analyzing multiple terrain and environmental parameters that influence slope stability. These parameters are inherently spatial, making Geographic Information Systems (GIS) an essential platform for such assessments. The integration of satellite imagery, digital elevation models (DEMs), meteorological data, and land cover information allows for a detailed spatial analysis of landslide susceptibility.

Using geospatial tools in landslide prediction facilitates:

- **Hazard mapping:** Identifying zones with varying levels of landslide risk to prioritize mitigation.
- **Mitigation planning:** Informing infrastructure design and development policies to reduce vulnerability to landslides.
- **Resource allocation:** Guiding emergency response efforts during disaster events to areas with the greatest need.

Furthermore, coupling geospatial analysis with machine learning models enhances predictive accuracy and helps automate the identification of potential landslide zones. It allows researchers to move beyond traditional qualitative assessments and develop replicable, scalable models suitable for large-scale analysis. This integration creates a synergistic effect, where data-driven insights support better risk reduction strategies and proactive environmental governance.

9.3   Landslide Conditioning Factors

Landslide conditioning factors are variables that describe the environmental conditions contributing to slope instability. These include geomorphological, hydrological, climatic, and anthropogenic factors. For this study, a combination of topographic, land cover, and climatic datasets was used.

These variables provide both direct and indirect indicators of slope stability. By evaluating the spatial distribution of these factors and their correlations with known landslide occurrences, a susceptibility model can be effectively trained. The relationship among these variables is often complex, necessitating the use of advanced statistical and machine learning techniques to identify patterns and interactions.

The selected factors for the Raigad region include:

- **Slope and Aspect:** Steep slopes increase gravitational force on soil particles, contributing to instability, while slope aspect influences microclimatic conditions like sunlight and moisture which can affect soil dryness or saturation.
- **Curvature:** Profile and plan curvature determine the direction and accumulation of surface runoff, which may promote erosion or waterlogging, both contributing to instability.
- **Elevation:** Elevation governs not only rainfall distribution but also soil development, vegetation type, and temperature variation—all of which influence slope stability.
- **NDVI (Normalized Difference Vegetation Index):** NDVI values derived from remote sensing data indicate vegetation health and coverage; higher NDVI values imply better root structure, which helps in anchoring the soil.
- **Precipitation:** Short-term rainfall events can trigger landslides, especially when soils are already saturated. High-intensity rainfall increases pore water pressure and reduces soil shear strength.
- **Annual Precipitation:** Long-term precipitation records reflect climatic trends that may influence cumulative soil moisture content and slope weakening over time.
- **LULC (Land Use/Land Cover):** LULC maps help identify land use patterns such as agriculture, urbanization, or forest cover, which affect the infiltration and runoff characteristics of the landscape.

9.4   Research Objectives

The primary aim of this research is to leverage geospatial data and machine learning techniques to enhance landslide susceptibility mapping in Raigad district. The specific

Table 9.1: Description of Geospatial Conditioning Factors

Factor	Description
Slope	Gradient of terrain surface; higher slope often implies higher landslide risk.
Aspect	Orientation of slope; south-facing slopes in the northern hemisphere receive more sunlight and may dry out faster.
Curvature	Convex or concave shape of the land affecting water flow and accumulation.
NDVI	Vegetation index derived from remote sensing data; low NDVI indicates less vegetation cover.
Elevation	Altitude above sea level; affects rainfall, vegetation type, and erosion.
Annual Precipitation	Cumulative rainfall over the year; contributes to prolonged soil saturation.
LULC	Land use/land cover types; urban areas and deforested zones have higher susceptibility.

objectives are:

(1) Prepare a comprehensive landslide conditioning dataset for Raigad district by integrating DEMs, land cover information, and meteorological records.

(2) Develop and train a Multi-Layer Perceptron model for classifying land areas based on landslide risk levels.

(3) Categorize areas into low, moderate, and high-risk zones to facilitate targeted planning and mitigation.

(4) Analyze the relation between recent LULC changes and the spatial distribution of landslide-prone zones.

9.5 Methodology

9.5.1 Study Area and Data Collection

Raigad district, located along the Konkan coast of Maharashtra, is characterized by a complex terrain comprising hills, plateaus, and river basins. Due to its varied topography and heavy seasonal monsoon rainfall, it has been prone to several landslide events in the past two decades.

In this study, the selection of the study area is motivated by both historical landslide records and the district's environmental sensitivity. A comprehensive dataset was curated using multiple geospatial sources. Digital Elevation Models (DEMs) were used for deriving slope, aspect, and curvature layers. Remote sensing data from Sentinel and Landsat missions

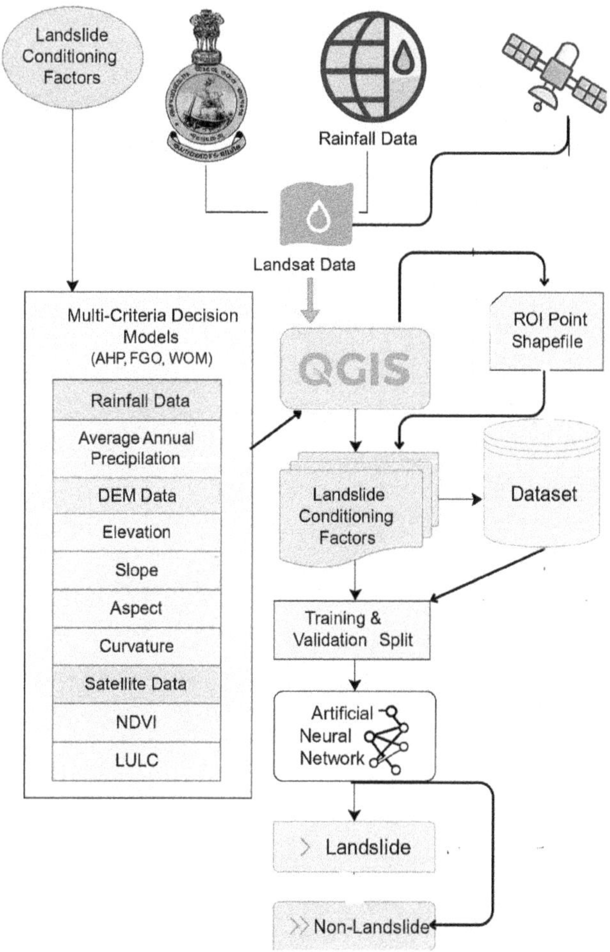

Figure 9.1: Workflow for Landslide Susceptibility Mapping Dataset Preparation

provided NDVI and LULC information. Meteorological data, including annual precipitation and intensity of rainfall events, were obtained from the Indian Meteorological Department (IMD). Historical landslide incident points, acquired from disaster management records, served as ground truth references.

9.5.2 Data Preprocessing

To ensure model accuracy and spatial consistency, the geospatial layers were subjected to several preprocessing steps. Each raster dataset was clipped to the boundary of Raigad district and resampled to a uniform pixel resolution. Cloudy and noisy pixels in satellite imagery were masked using quality assurance bands and visual inspection.

All layers were then normalized using min-max scaling, ensuring that the input features fed into the machine learning model were on a common scale. Geospatial alignment and projection correction were performed using QGIS to ensure overlay accuracy. Landslide location points were geocoded and transformed into binary labels, signifying susceptible and non-susceptible regions based on historical occurrence.

9.5.3 Model Development

The classification problem was approached using a Multi-Layer Perceptron (MLP) – a form of feed-forward neural network well-suited for tabular datasets. The architecture consisted of one hidden layer containing six neurons activated using the ReLU function. The output layer had three neurons corresponding to risk classes – low, moderate, and high – and used the softmax activation function to handle multi-class prediction.

The model employed categorical cross-entropy as its loss function, optimized using the Adam optimizer. The dataset was randomly divided into training (80%) and testing (20%) subsets, and one-hot encoding was applied to the target variable to match the multi-class framework. Training was carried out over 100 epochs, and early stopping was implemented to prevent overfitting.

9.5.4 Training and Evaluation

The model was trained using the normalized geospatial conditioning factors as input. Evaluation metrics included accuracy, precision, recall, and F1-score, providing a comprehensive view of the model's performance. A confusion matrix was plotted to visualize class-wise prediction capability.

9.6 Results and Discussion

9.6.1 Model Performance

Table 9.2: MLP Performance on Raigad Landslide Dataset

Metric	Accuracy	Precision	Recall	F1 Score
Value	95%	100%	95%	97.43%

The MLP model exhibited strong generalization, classifying most of the test points accurately. Its high precision value indicates a low false-positive rate, which is critical for real-world application in disaster-prone areas where overestimating risk could lead to unnecessary allocation of resources.

9.6.2 Landslide Risk Zones

The classified output maps delineated the district into three risk zones:

- **Low Risk:** Dominated by regions with gentle slopes, high NDVI values, and dense vegetation cover.
- **Moderate Risk:** Found mostly in transitional zones with moderate slope gradients and limited forest cover.
- **High Risk:** Concentrated in areas with steep slopes, barren or urban land cover, and high rainfall intensity.

These maps are instrumental for planning and mitigation, as they allow government authorities to focus resources on high-risk areas while monitoring changes in moderate zones.

9.7 Summary

- A machine learning-based landslide susceptibility mapping study was conducted for Raigad district using MLP classifiers.
- Multiple geospatial datasets were integrated, including DEMs, LULC maps, NDVI, and precipitation layers.
- The trained model showed high classification accuracy and revealed clear spatial patterns of susceptibility.
- LULC and slope were the dominant contributing factors, although NDVI did not show a statistically strong correlation with landslide occurrence.
- The approach outlined is reproducible and can be adapted for similar landscapes across the Western Ghats.

Exercise Questions

(1) What are the primary conditioning factors that influence landslide susceptibility?
(2) Explain how NDVI and LULC influence slope stability.
(3) Describe the architecture and training process of a Multi-Layer Perceptron used in this study.
(4) What conclusions can be drawn from the confusion matrix of the MLP classifier?

Notes and Suggestions

- This chapter was developed based on original research conducted during the author's Ph.D. work in Raigad district.

- Students are encouraged to replicate this study using Google Earth Engine and public datasets to explore real-time mapping possibilities.
- Field validation is essential to ground-truth the model predictions and improve the robustness of geospatial models.
- Integration with socio-economic data and infrastructure layers may further enhance hazard planning strategies.

Chapter 10

Black Spot Classification Using Machine Learning – A Case Study from Raigad District

Learning Objectives

At the end of this chapter, you should be able to:

- Understand the significance of black spot detection as a geospatial task.
- Learn how accident data can be used to classify high-risk road zones.
- Explore machine learning algorithms for binary classification.
- Analyze a real-world accident dataset from Raigad using Python and scikit-learn.
- Evaluate classification models using precision, recall, F1-score, and AUC.

10.1 Introduction

Road accidents continue to be a pressing concern in India, causing over 150,000 fatalities annually. Identifying high-risk road segments, or *black spots*, is essential to improving safety. Raigad District, with its growing vehicular traffic and complex road networks, faces a significant number of traffic accidents.

Traditional approaches to black spot identification rely on manual analysis of accident records.

This study, a part of the author's Ph.D. work, proposes an automated, geospatially-informed machine learning approach for the classification of accident locations into black spots using official traffic data from Raigad district.

10.2   Significance of Black Spot Detection as a Geospatial Task

Black spot detection provides multiple benefits:

- **Public Safety:** Enables timely preventive measures.
- **Urban Planning:** Helps in designing safer roads.
- **Insurance:** Identifies high-risk regions for risk analysis.
- **Legal Use:** Assists in accident verification and litigation through spatial evidence.

10.3   Research Objectives

(1) Develop an accident spot dataset using 2019–2021 records from Raigad Traffic Police.
(2) Create a black spot classifier model based on accident frequency and severity.
(3) Compare classification performance across multiple machine learning algorithms.

10.4   Material and Methods

10.4.1   Study Area

The study was conducted in the Raigad district of Maharashtra, India, a coastal region known for its tourism-driven traffic. With an increasing number of vehicles and human activity, this area frequently experiences road congestion and accidents. Identifying and classifying accident-prone locations (black spots) is crucial for implementing effective safety interventions.

10.4.2   Data Collection

Accident data was collected from 63 distinct locations within Raigad over a three-year period from 2019 to 2021. The dataset captures:

- Geographic coordinates (Latitude and Longitude)
- Annual number of accidents and fatalities for each year (2019–2021)
- Total number of accidents (TotA) and fatalities (TotF) across three years

Each location was labeled as a **black spot** (Label = 1) based on the following rule:

- It recorded **five or more accidents** over the three-year period, or
- It recorded **ten or more fatalities** over the same period

This threshold was chosen based on national and regional road safety guidelines.

Table 10.1: Sample Black Spot Dataset

Lat	Lon	A19	F19	A20	F20	A21	F21	TotA	TotF	Label
18.76	73.34	0	0	4	1	0	0	4	1	0
18.95	73.16	1	5	7	5	2	3	10	13	1

In this table, A19, A20, A21 represent the number of accidents in 2019, 2020, and 2021 respectively, while F19, F20, F21 represent the fatalities. TotA and TotF are computed as the sum across the years. The final binary label is determined using the threshold conditions mentioned above.

10.4.3 Preprocessing

Before training the models, the dataset underwent the following preprocessing steps:

- **Feature Scaling:** All numerical features were standardized using `StandardScaler` from `sklearn`, which scales the data to have zero mean and unit variance. This ensures uniform influence from all features during model training.
- **Train-Test Split:** The dataset was split into 70% for training and 30% for testing to evaluate generalization performance.
- **Cross Validation:** K-fold cross-validation was employed during training to ensure model robustness and to prevent overfitting.

10.4.4 Machine Learning Models Compared

To identify the most suitable classifier for black spot detection, five supervised learning algorithms were implemented:

- Logistic Regression
- Linear Discriminant Analysis (LDA)
- Naïve Bayes
- Support Vector Machine (SVM)
- Multi-Layer Perceptron (MLP)

All models were implemented using the `scikit-learn` Python library and executed on the Google Colab platform.

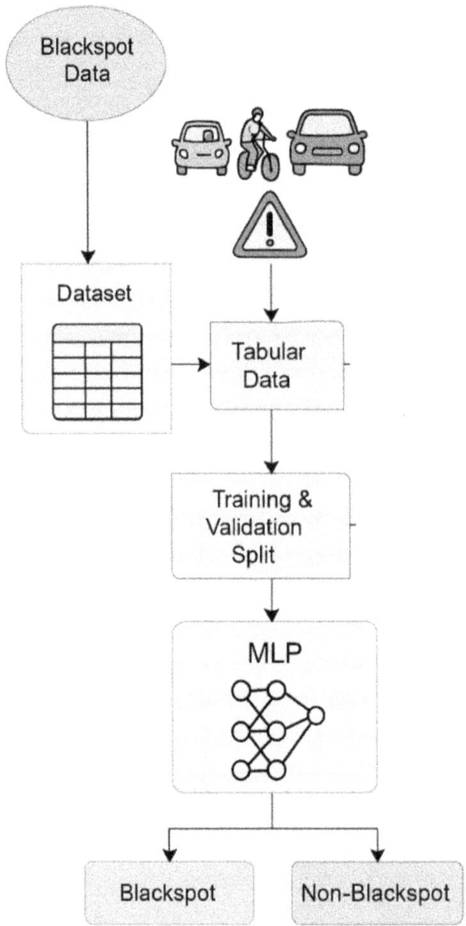

Figure 10.1: Workflow of Black Spot Classification Using MLP

10.4.5 MLP-Based Black Spot Classifier

Among the classifiers tested, the Multi-Layer Perceptron (MLP) model showed the highest overall performance. The MLP is a feedforward artificial neural network composed of multiple layers of interconnected neurons. It is particularly effective for binary classification problems when nonlinear relationships exist between the input features and the target class.

Model Inputs: The input layer received standardized accident-related features, including yearly and total accident/fatality counts.

Model Architecture:

- **Input Layer:** Receives all normalized features related to accident statistics.

- **Hidden Layers:** One or more layers of neurons apply weighted transformations followed by the ReLU (Rectified Linear Unit) activation function. ReLU helps capture non-linear interactions and accelerates convergence.
- **Output Layer:** A single neuron with Sigmoid activation was used to output a probability score, which was thresholded (typically at 0.5) to classify a location as black spot (1) or non-black spot (0).

Training Objective: The model was trained using binary cross-entropy loss, optimized via the Adam optimizer. Evaluation metrics included precision, recall, F1 score, and Area Under the ROC Curve (AUC) to assess classification quality.

10.5   Results and Discussion

10.5.1   Model Comparison

To assess the performance of various machine learning algorithms in classifying accident-prone locations (black spots), five supervised models were evaluated using the preprocessed dataset. These models included:

- Logistic Regression
- Linear Discriminant Analysis (LDA)
- Naïve Bayes
- Support Vector Machine (SVM)
- Multi-Layer Perceptron (MLP)

All models were trained using 70% of the dataset and tested on the remaining 30%, with performance evaluated using key classification metrics:

- **Training Accuracy (Train Acc.):** Accuracy on the training data—higher values indicate that the model has learned patterns in the data.
- **Testing Accuracy (Test Acc.):** Accuracy on unseen test data—critical for evaluating generalization.
- **Precision:** The percentage of locations predicted as black spots that were actually black spots. High precision means fewer false positives.
- **Recall:** The percentage of actual black spots that were correctly identified. High recall means fewer false negatives.
- **F1 Score:** Harmonic mean of precision and recall, useful when there's class imbalance.
- **AUC (Area Under the Curve):** Measures overall model performance; higher AUC means better discrimination between classes.

Table 10.2 summarizes the results across all models.

Table 10.2: Performance Metrics for ML Models

Model	Train Acc.	Test Acc.	Precision	Recall	F1 Score	AUC
Logistic Regression	97.14%	95.56%	100%	87.5%	93.33%	0.9375
LDA	77.14%	75.56%	100%	31.25%	47.62%	0.6562
Naïve Bayes	79.05%	84.44%	100%	56.25%	72.00%	0.7812
SVM	97.14%	95.56%	100%	87.5%	93.33%	0.9375
MLP	96.19%	**97.78%**	100%	**93.75%**	**96.77%**	**0.9688**

Discussion

Among all models, the MLP achieved the best performance across almost all metrics. With a test accuracy of 97.78%, precision of 100%, recall of 93.75%, and an F1 score of 96.77%, the MLP classifier not only learned the patterns effectively but also generalized well to unseen data. This suggests that the model was successful in balancing both false positives and false negatives, which is particularly important in safety-critical tasks like black spot identification.

Logistic Regression and SVM also performed well, but their slightly lower recall values (87.5%) indicate that some black spots were missed. LDA and Naïve Bayes, on the other hand, showed relatively weaker performance, especially in recall, implying that they struggled with capturing the complex feature relationships in the data.

The high AUC of the MLP (0.9688) further confirms its robust discrimination capability between black spot and non-black spot locations.

Thus, the MLP model proved to be the most effective classifier for this task, making it a suitable choice for practical deployment in road safety monitoring systems.

10.5.2   Hypothesis Test – Black Spot and Geospatial Factors

Hypothesis testing is a fundamental aspect of statistical analysis, aimed at determining whether there is sufficient evidence to support a specific belief about a dataset. In the context of black spot classification, it is essential to assess whether certain features—such as accident severity, number of fatalities, or location characteristics—are statistically associated with the occurrence of a black spot.

By conducting hypothesis testing, specifically the Chi-Square Test of Independence, we can objectively verify whether observed differences between black spot and non-black spot locations are likely due to random variation or indicate a meaningful relationship.

10.5.3 Chi-Square Test of Independence

The Chi-Square Test of Independence is a non-parametric test used to evaluate whether two categorical variables are associated.

In this study, the two variables considered are:

- Whether a location is classified as a black spot (Yes/No).
- Attributes such as total number of accidents, number of serious injuries, number of fatalities, and accident severity.

Null Hypothesis (H_0): There is no association between the selected features and the occurrence of black spots. Any observed differences are purely due to random chance.

Alternative Hypothesis (H_1): There is a significant association between the selected features and the occurrence of black spots.

10.5.4 Application to the Current Study

In this case study, accident data collected from **Raigad Traffic Police records** for the period 2019–2021 was used. The accident attributes were analyzed to test whether they have a statistically significant association with black spot classification.

The test was performed following these steps:

(1) Accident data was classified into two groups: "Black Spot" and "Not a Black Spot."
(2) Contingency tables were constructed for features like the number of fatalities and total accidents.
(3) The Chi-Square statistic and corresponding p-value were computed.
(4) The results were evaluated at a significance level of $\alpha = 0.05$.

10.5.5 Interpretation of Results

The Chi-Square test produced the following results:

- Chi-square value: 4.415
- p-value: 0.0356
- Critical value at $\alpha = 0.05$: 3.841

Since the p-value was less than 0.05, we **reject the null hypothesis**. This indicates that there is a statistically significant association between the selected accident attributes and the occurrence of black spots in Raigad district.

10.5.6 Implications of the Result

- Accident features such as high fatality counts and high accident frequencies are significantly associated with black spot classification.
- This validates that geospatial and accident data can be reliably used to model and predict high-risk road segments.
- Policymakers and traffic authorities can prioritize road safety interventions at locations statistically identified as black spots.

10.6 Summary

- A black spot classification model was successfully developed using Raigad accident data.
- Among all algorithms, MLP achieved the best performance (97.78% accuracy).
- The model can aid authorities in proactive black spot monitoring.
- Statistical testing confirmed geospatial relevance of accident-prone areas.

Exercise Questions

(1) What is the significance of identifying black spots using geospatial analysis?
(2) Explain the criteria used by the Raigad police for marking black spots.
(3) Describe the preprocessing steps used before training the ML models.
(4) Which ML model gave the best performance and why?
(5) Discuss the outcome of the chi-square hypothesis test.
(6) Discuss the significance of p-values in the hypothesis testing conducted in this study.

Notes and Suggestions

- Future work may integrate weather and traffic data for real-time prediction.
- Spatial clustering methods like DBSCAN can enhance hotspot identification.
- Web GIS dashboards could visualize black spots dynamically.

Part IV

Emerging Frontiers and Vision

Chapter 11

Geospatial AI for Climate Action and Sustainability

Learning Objectives

At the end of this chapter, you should be able to:

- Understand the role of Geospatial AI in addressing climate change and promoting sustainability.
- Explore applications of Geospatial AI in key sectors such as agriculture, forestry, and water resources.
- Learn how to integrate deep learning (DL) technologies with policy frameworks and the Sustainable Development Goals (SDGs).
- Gain insight into real-world case studies demonstrating the impact of Geospatial AI on climate action and sustainability.

11.1   Introduction

Climate change and environmental degradation are some of the most pressing challenges of the 21st century. As global populations grow and natural resources continue to be strained, addressing these challenges requires innovative solutions that are both scalable and sustainable. Geospatial AI, which combines geospatial data with artificial intelligence and machine learning techniques, offers powerful tools for addressing climate change impacts and promoting sustainable development. This chapter explores the applications of Geospatial AI in key sectors, including agriculture, forestry, and water resources, while also discussing how these technologies can be aligned with policy frameworks and the SDGs.

11.2 Geospatial AI in Agriculture

Agriculture is both a significant contributor to climate change and one of the sectors most affected by its impacts. Geospatial AI offers transformative solutions for sustainable farming practices, improving crop yield predictions, and mitigating environmental impacts.

Applications

- **Precision Agriculture**: Using satellite imagery, remote sensing, and deep learning, farmers can monitor crop health, predict yields, and identify pests or diseases in real-time.
- **Soil Health Monitoring**: AI models can analyze soil moisture, temperature, and nutrient levels to provide actionable insights for sustainable land management.
- **Climate-resilient Crop Selection**: Geospatial AI can help in selecting crop varieties that are better suited to specific climates, helping farmers adapt to shifting weather patterns.

Case Study: AI for Climate-Smart Agriculture

An AI system developed by a consortium of universities and companies uses satellite data to help farmers in East Africa make better decisions regarding irrigation and crop rotation, resulting in improved yields and reduced water usage.

Mini-Project Idea

Title: Predicting Crop Yield Using NDVI and Machine Learning Regression

Objective: Use NDVI time-series data and rainfall parameters to train a regression model that estimates crop yield for a specific crop (e.g., rice or wheat).

Tools: Google Earth Engine, Python (scikit-learn), QGIS

Data: Sentinel-2 imagery, India Meteorological Department (IMD) rainfall data, district-wise crop yield statistics (from agri.gov.in)

Outcome: Yield prediction maps at the block or district level with error metrics and correlation to actual production data.

11.3 Geospatial AI in Forestry

Forests are critical for carbon sequestration, biodiversity conservation, and maintaining the global climate balance. However, they are also under threat from deforestation, forest degradation, and climate change.

Applications

- **Deforestation Monitoring**: AI-powered algorithms can analyze satellite imagery to detect and monitor deforestation in real-time, enabling rapid response to illegal logging activities.
- **Forest Carbon Stock Estimation**: Geospatial AI can estimate the amount of carbon stored in forests, providing valuable data for carbon trading systems and climate policy.
- **Forest Fire Prediction**: Using machine learning and remote sensing data, AI models can predict the occurrence of forest fires based on environmental factors like temperature, humidity, and vegetation type.

Case Study: Monitoring Deforestation in the Amazon

Using a combination of remote sensing, AI, and cloud computing, researchers have been able to monitor deforestation in the Amazon rainforest on a large scale. This system helps inform policies and efforts to curb illegal logging activities.

Mini-Project Idea

Title: Detecting Deforestation and Forest Fragmentation Using Deep Learning and Sentinel Imagery

Objective: Train a CNN-based classifier to detect deforested areas in a forest reserve and assess changes over the last 5 years.

Tools: TensorFlow/Keras, Sentinel-2, QGIS, Google Earth Engine

Data: Sentinel-2 images (multi-year), forest boundaries (Forest Survey of India), high-resolution imagery (Google Earth for validation)

Outcome: A binary map of deforestation, forest fragmentation index, and comparison with official forest loss statistics.

11.4 Geospatial AI in Water Resources

Water is essential for all life on Earth, and its management is crucial to sustainable development. Climate change is making water availability more unpredictable, especially in regions prone to droughts or flooding.

Applications

- **Water Quality Monitoring**: Geospatial AI can be used to analyze satellite data to detect water quality issues, such as algae blooms or contamination from industrial waste.
- **Flood Risk Prediction**: AI models integrated with GIS can predict flood risks in real-time by analyzing weather patterns, topography, and historical flood data.
- **Water Resource Management**: AI can optimize the allocation of water resources for agriculture, industry, and domestic use, ensuring equitable distribution and efficient use.

Case Study: Flood Prediction in the Ganges River Basin

A Geospatial AI model developed for the Ganges River Basin uses remote sensing data and hydrological models to predict seasonal flooding, enabling early warning systems for affected communities.

Mini-Project Idea

Title: Monitoring Reservoir Storage Using SAR Imagery and Surface Water Detection Models

Objective: Automate surface water extraction from Sentinel-1 SAR data to track seasonal water level changes in major reservoirs.

Tools: Google Earth Engine, Python, SNAP toolbox

Data: Sentinel-1 (for water mapping), WRIS waterbody shapefiles, rainfall data (IMD)

Outcome: Seasonal surface area change graphs, a map showing declining water trends, and correlation with rainfall deficit periods.

11.5 Integrating Deep Learning with Policy Frameworks and the SDGs

The Sustainable Development Goals (SDGs) adopted by the United Nations aim to address the world's most pressing environmental, social, and economic challenges by 2030. Geospatial

AI, particularly deep learning, plays a critical role in achieving these goals, especially in areas related to climate action, clean water, and life on land.

Integrating DL with Policy

- **Climate Action (SDG 13)**: Deep learning can be applied to understand the impacts of climate change, predict future trends, and inform mitigation and adaptation policies.
- **Life on Land (SDG 15)**: AI can be used for monitoring biodiversity, combating deforestation, and supporting sustainable land management practices.
- **Water Management (SDG 6)**: Geospatial AI can support policies for water conservation, water quality monitoring, and efficient water resource management.

Example

Governments can use AI-driven models to analyze geospatial data and assess the effectiveness of policies aimed at achieving SDG targets. For example, a deep learning model analyzing satellite images can evaluate the impact of forest conservation policies by measuring changes in land cover over time.

Mini-Project Idea

Title: Creating a Geospatial Dashboard for SDG 13: Climate Action Using Open Datasets

Objective: Develop a dashboard (static or interactive) that visualizes geospatial indicators such as deforestation, crop loss, UHI intensity, or water stress in relation to SDG 13 targets.

Tools: Python (Dash/Streamlit), GEE, QGIS, Power BI (optional)

Data: Multisource — Forest loss (Global Forest Watch), Water scarcity (India WRIS), Urban growth (MODIS LULC), IMD temperature data

Outcome: A prototype geospatial policy dashboard with recommendations aligned to SDG indicators, suitable for decision-makers or NGOs.

11.6 Deep Learning Algorithm Selection for Geospatial AI Applications

Following table suggests deep learning algorithms best suited for a specific Geospatial AI application.

Geospatial AI Application	Recommended Deep Learning Algorithm	Reason for Selection
Precision Agriculture	Convolutional Neural Networks (CNNs)	CNNs excel in image processing tasks, such as analyzing satellite images for crop health and yield prediction.
Soil Health Monitoring	Recurrent Neural Networks (RNNs)	RNNs can process time-series data from sensors to model soil moisture and nutrient levels over time.
Deforestation Monitoring	U-Net (Segmentation Model)	U-Net is ideal for pixel-wise classification tasks such as detecting deforestation or forest cover changes in satellite images.
Forest Carbon Stock Estimation	Fully Convolutional Networks (FCNs)	FCNs are useful for segmentation and estimating continuous variables like carbon stock distribution in forests.
Flood Risk Prediction	Long Short-Term Memory Networks (LSTMs)	LSTMs are effective for sequential data, such as time-series weather data, to predict flooding risks.
Water Quality Monitoring	CNNs or Deep Neural Networks (DNNs)	CNNs can classify water quality from remote sensing images, while DNNs can handle structured data for contamination analysis.

11.7 Challenges and Future Directions

While the potential of Geospatial AI for climate action and sustainability is vast, there are still significant challenges to overcome:

- **Data Accessibility and Quality**: High-quality, high-resolution geospatial data is critical for training accurate AI models. However, such data can be difficult to obtain or expensive, especially in developing regions.
- **Model Generalization**: Deep learning models trained on data from one region may not always perform well in another region due to variations in climate, land cover, or socioeconomic factors.

- **Ethical and Social Impacts**: AI applications must be designed with consideration for their ethical implications, especially regarding privacy, data security, and the potential displacement of local knowledge.

Future advancements in Geospatial AI for climate action will likely focus on improving model accuracy, enhancing the accessibility of geospatial data, and developing more user-friendly tools for decision-makers.

11.8   Conclusion

Geospatial AI holds significant promise for advancing climate action and sustainability. By providing powerful tools for monitoring, predicting, and mitigating the impacts of climate change, Geospatial AI can support sustainable development across sectors such as agriculture, forestry, and water resources. The integration of deep learning with policy frameworks and the SDGs is essential to ensure that these technologies contribute to achieving global climate goals.

Exercise Questions

(1) How can Geospatial AI be used to predict crop yields in a specific region using satellite imagery?
(2) Discuss the role of AI in deforestation monitoring and how it can assist in policy enforcement.
(3) Explain how AI models can be integrated with SDG frameworks to monitor progress on climate-related targets.
(4) What challenges do you foresee in applying Geospatial AI in developing countries for climate action?

Notes and Suggestions

- **Pro Tip**: When working with AI models for climate-related applications, always ensure that the model is regularly updated with new data to account for changing environmental conditions.
- **Real-World Applications**: Look for open-source datasets from platforms like Google Earth Engine to practice working with geospatial data for climate action projects.
- **Future Learning**: Explore specialized machine learning techniques, such as reinforcement learning, for dynamic resource management in agriculture and water resources.

Chapter 12

Future Directions and Student Research Opportunities

Learning Objectives

At the end of this chapter, you should be able to:

- **Understand the concepts of federated learning, multisensor fusion, and edge computing in the context of geospatial AI.**
- **Learn how federated learning can help in handling sensitive geospatial data while preserving privacy.**
- **Discover how combining multiple sensors (multisensor fusion) can enhance geospatial analysis.**
- **Understand how edge computing can provide real-time solutions for geospatial AI systems.**
- **Explore future trends and emerging technologies in geospatial AI.**

12.1 Introduction

Geospatial AI, the fusion of artificial intelligence with geospatial data, is evolving rapidly. New technologies and methods are continually being developed to enhance the capabilities of AI in geospatial applications. Among these, **federated learning**, **multisensor fusion**, and **edge computing** hold immense potential. This chapter introduces these technologies, explaining their applications, challenges, and how they can be integrated into geospatial AI for future advancements.

12.2 Federated Learning for Sensitive Geospatial Data

12.2.1 What is Federated Learning?

Federated learning is a technique that allows machine learning models to be trained across many devices or systems, without needing to share data between them. Instead of sending data to a central server for processing, the model is trained directly on the device (or at the data source) and only the model updates are shared. This is especially important for protecting sensitive data.

12.2.2 How Does Federated Learning Help in Geospatial AI?

In geospatial AI, federated learning can be applied to situations where data privacy is important. For example:

- **Mobile Devices:** Geospatial apps on smartphones can use federated learning to improve location-based services (like navigation or traffic prediction) without sending sensitive user data to the cloud.
- **Remote Sensing:** Satellites and drones can generate vast amounts of geospatial data. Federated learning allows models to be trained locally on these devices, minimizing the need to transmit large data volumes back to central servers.

12.2.3 Benefits of Federated Learning

- **Data Privacy:** The most important benefit is that sensitive geospatial data, such as personal locations or information from remote sensors, never leaves the local device, ensuring privacy.
- **Efficient Use of Resources:** Federated learning makes use of the computational power of distributed devices, reducing the need for powerful central servers.

12.2.4 Challenges and Research Opportunities

- **Data Heterogeneity:** Different devices may have different data formats, making it hard to combine them for training.
- **Model Convergence:** Training across distributed devices may result in slower model improvement due to limited data on each device.

Research Focus: Future work can focus on making federated learning more efficient, especially in handling the diversity of data from various geospatial devices.

12.3 Multisensor Fusion in Geospatial AI

12.3.1 What is Multisensor Fusion?

Multisensor fusion is the process of combining data from multiple types of sensors to create more accurate, reliable, and comprehensive information. For example, combining satellite imagery, drone data, and weather sensors can provide a more complete picture of a particular area.

12.3.2 How Does Multisensor Fusion Work in Geospatial AI?

Geospatial data can come from many different sources, each offering different perspectives. For example:

- **Satellites:** Provide high-resolution images of the Earth's surface.
- **Drones:** Offer detailed, up-close data of specific areas.
- **Ground Sensors:** Can measure temperature, humidity, or soil moisture.

By combining these different data types, we can make more accurate predictions and analyses. For instance, in **land use and land cover classification**, combining high-resolution satellite images with ground-based observations can improve classification accuracy.

12.3.3 Benefits of Multisensor Fusion

- **Enhanced Accuracy:** By combining data from multiple sources, you get a more complete and precise picture of the environment.
- **Robustness:** Different sensors may perform well under different conditions. For example, radar is useful in poor weather conditions, while optical imagery is useful under clear skies.
- **Better Decision Making:** Multisensor fusion helps in decision-making, particularly in **disaster management**, **urban planning**, and **agriculture**.

12.3.4 Challenges and Research Opportunities

- **Data Alignment:** Sensors may operate at different times or resolutions, making it difficult to align the data accurately.

- **Data Overload:** The amount of data generated by multiple sensors can be overwhelming. Efficient methods are needed for processing and analyzing large datasets.

Research Focus: Researchers are focusing on developing more sophisticated algorithms for combining multisensor data and managing large datasets efficiently.

12.4 Edge Computing for Geospatial AI

12.4.1 What is Edge Computing?

Edge computing refers to processing data close to its source (e.g., on IoT devices, mobile phones, or sensors) rather than sending it to centralized servers. This reduces the time it takes to process data and can improve the responsiveness of geospatial AI systems.

12.4.2 How Does Edge Computing Benefit Geospatial AI?

In traditional systems, geospatial data is collected by sensors, sent to a central server, and processed there. In edge computing, data is processed directly on the device or at the location where it is collected, which is crucial for applications requiring real-time data processing.

For example:

- **Autonomous Vehicles:** Edge computing enables vehicles to process geospatial data from their sensors (like GPS, LiDAR, and cameras) in real-time, helping them make instant decisions for navigation.
- **Disaster Response:** During natural disasters, edge computing allows drones or IoT sensors to process geospatial data on-site, helping emergency responders make faster decisions.

12.4.3 Benefits of Edge Computing

- **Real-time Processing:** With edge computing, data can be processed instantly, which is essential for applications like traffic management or emergency response.
- **Reduced Latency:** By processing data locally, edge computing reduces the time delay (latency) associated with sending data to a centralized server.
- **Efficient Use of Bandwidth:** Edge computing reduces the need to transfer large amounts of data to central servers, making it ideal for environments with limited internet bandwidth.

12.4.4 Challenges and Research Opportunities

- **Limited Computational Power:** Edge devices often have less computational power than central servers, which can limit the complexity of the AI models that can be deployed.
- **Security:** Processing data at the edge increases the risk of data breaches and security issues, particularly in sensitive geospatial applications.

Research Focus: Future research can focus on optimizing edge devices for better computational efficiency and addressing security concerns.

12.5 Summary

In this chapter, we explored the integration of federated learning, multisensor fusion, and edge computing into geospatial AI, highlighting their significant potential for the future. These technologies offer several advantages, such as enhancing privacy through federated learning, improving data accuracy via multisensor fusion, and enabling real-time decision-making with edge computing. The application of these technologies is particularly beneficial in areas like disaster management, urban planning, and agriculture, where timely and accurate information is crucial. As these technologies continue to evolve, they are expected to play a pivotal role in shaping the future of geospatial intelligence, making it more efficient, accurate, and accessible to a broader range of users and applications.

12.6 Exercise Questions

(1) Explain the concept of **federated learning**. How does it help in protecting sensitive geospatial data?
(2) What is **multisensor fusion**, and why is it important in geospatial data analysis?
(3) Describe how **edge computing** improves real-time decision-making in autonomous vehicles.
(4) What challenges do researchers face when implementing federated learning in geospatial AI systems?
(5) How can **multisensor fusion** be applied in disaster management to improve response times and accuracy?

12.7 Notes and Suggestions

- **Pro Tip:** When working with **federated learning**, make sure that the models you build are robust enough to handle data from various sources with different characteristics.
- **Real-World Example: Autonomous vehicles** rely heavily on **edge computing** to process data from sensors like GPS, cameras, and LiDAR in real-time. This enables them to make immediate decisions while driving.
- **Further Exploration:** If you are interested in **multisensor fusion**, look into how satellite data is integrated with ground-based sensors for monitoring agricultural practices in precision farming.

Appendix A

About the Author

Dr. Geetanjali Sameer Mahamunkar is a Lecturer at Dr. Babasaheb Ambedkar Technological University, Lonere. She holds a Ph.D. in Computer Engineering, with her research focused on deep learning techniques for geospatial data analysis. Her academic expertise spans artificial intelligence, GIS, and remote sensing. She has authored multiple research publications in reputed journals and conferences and has contributed to book chapter on deep learning applications. She has also served as the Coordinator for the M.Tech. program in Remote Sensing and GIS and has extensive experience in teaching, research, and academic administration. She can be reached at gsmahamunkar@dbatu.ac.in. For postal correspondence: Department of Computer Engineering, Dr. Babasaheb Ambedkar Technological University, Lonere, Dist. Raigad (MS) 402103.

Appendix B

Abbreviations

Following is the list of commonly used abbreviations referenced throughout this book.

AI Artificial Intelligence

ANN Artificial Neural Network

AUC-ROC Area Under Curve – Receiver Operating Characteristic

BRDF Bidirectional Reflectance Distribution Function

CNN Convolutional Neural Network

CRS Coordinate Reference System

DEM Digital Elevation Model

DL Deep Learning

EO Earth Observation

ESA European Space Agency

ETL Extract, Transform, Load

GAN Generative Adversarial Network

GEE Google Earth Engine

GIS Geographic Information System

GPS Global Positioning System

GRU Gated Recurrent Unit

IoU Intersection over Union

IPR Intellectual Property Rights

KML Keyhole Markup Language

LiDAR Light Detection and Ranging

LULC Land Use Land Cover

MAE Mean Absolute Error

ML Machine Learning

MLP Multilayer Perceptron

MODIS Moderate Resolution Imaging Spectroradiometer

MSE Mean Squared Error

NDVI Normalized Difference Vegetation Index

NASA National Aeronautics and Space Administration

NIR Near Infrared

NOAA National Oceanic and Atmospheric Administration

OSM OpenStreetMap

PCA Principal Component Analysis

RNN Recurrent Neural Network

SAR Synthetic Aperture Radar

SDG Sustainable Development Goal

SGD Stochastic Gradient Descent

SVM Support Vector Machine

TIF/TIFF Tagged Image File Format

UAV Unmanned Aerial Vehicle

UN United Nations

USGS United States Geological Survey

WGS84 World Geodetic System 1984

WMS Web Map Service

XML Extensible Markup Language

Appendix C

Recommended Datasets and Open Tools

Remote Sensing Datasets

- **Landsat Series (USGS)** – Free multispectral satellite imagery from 1972 to present.
  https://earthexplorer.usgs.gov/
- **Sentinel Data (ESA)** – High-resolution optical and radar data from Sentinel-1, 2, and 3 missions.
  https://scihub.copernicus.eu/
- [MODIS:] Moderate Resolution Imaging Spectroradiometer data from NASA.
  https://modis.gsfc.nasa.gov/data/
- **India WRIS (Water Resources Information System)** – Government data for water bodies and hydrological studies.
  https://indiawris.gov.in/
- **Bhuvan (ISRO)** – National geospatial portal with thematic layers for India.
  https://bhuvan.nrsc.gov.in/
- **Raigad LULC maps for the year 2002 to 2021.** figshare. Figure. https://doi.org/10.6084/m9.figshare.24146190.v1
- **Dataset for Binary Image Classification of Mangroves**, Mendeley Data, V1, https://doi.org/10.17632/ss5t249wdp.1
- **Dataset for Landslide Susceptibility Prediction**, Mendeley Data, V1, https://doi.org/10.17632/jsn8cwb9nz.1

Geospatial Software and Tools

- **QGIS** – Free and open-source GIS desktop application.
  https://qgis.org/
- **Google Earth Engine (GEE)** – Cloud-based platform for planetary-scale geospatial analysis.
  https://earthengine.google.com/
- **SNAP (Sentinel Application Platform)** – Tool from ESA for processing Sentinel data.
  https://step.esa.int/main/toolboxes/snap/
- **Radiant MLHub** – Repository of labeled training datasets for geospatial machine learning.
  https://mlhub.earth/
- **OpenStreetMap (OSM)** – Community-driven vector data for roads, buildings, and natural features.
  https://www.openstreetmap.org/

Python Libraries for Spatial AI

- `rasterio`, `geopandas`, `shapely` – Core libraries for geospatial data handling.
- `tensorflow`, `keras`, `pytorch` – Deep learning frameworks.
- `scikit-learn`, `xgboost` – Baseline ML models.
- `matplotlib`, `seaborn`, `plotly` – Visualization.

Appendix D

Glossary

Geospatial Data: Data that includes geographic components such as coordinates, shape, or spatial reference.

Remote Sensing: The science of obtaining information about objects or areas from a distance, typically from aircraft or satellites.

Raster Data: Grid-based spatial data in which each pixel holds a value representing information, such as temperature or elevation.

Vector Data: Spatial data represented using points, lines, and polygons to model real-world features.

Convolutional Neural Network (CNN): A type of deep learning model designed for analyzing visual data through convolution operations.

Recurrent Neural Network (RNN): A neural network with feedback loops, suited for temporal or sequential data analysis.

Transfer Learning: A deep learning technique that uses pre-trained models on new tasks, reducing the need for large datasets.

IoU (Intersection over Union): A metric to evaluate segmentation models by comparing predicted and actual overlap.

Differential Privacy: A technique to ensure individual data cannot be reverse-engineered from aggregated datasets.

Open Science: A practice of making research outputs (data, models, code) freely available and reproducible.

Digital Twin Earth: A virtual representation of Earth processes used for simulation, analysis, and decision support.

Appendix E

Mini-Project Ideas and Student Worksheets

This appendix provides a collection of self-contained, hands-on mini-project worksheets designed to support students in applying concepts from Chapter 11 *Geospatial AI for Climate Action and Sustainability*. Each worksheet outlines objectives, tools, datasets, and expected outcomes to facilitate undergraduate or graduate-level exploration of real-world environmental problems using geospatial AI techniques.

Mini-Project 1: Geospatial AI in Agriculture

Project Title:

Predicting Crop Yield Using NDVI and Machine Learning Regression

Background & Motivation:

Monitoring and forecasting crop yields is essential for food security. This project uses NDVI and rainfall data to build a model that estimates yields of a selected crop.

Objective:

Train a regression model to estimate crop yields using vegetation indices and climatic inputs.

Tools & Technologies:

Google Earth Engine, Python (scikit-learn), QGIS

Datasets Required:

- Sentinel-2 NDVI
- Rainfall data (India Meteorological Department)
- Crop yield data (agri.gov.in or local government sources)

Workflow Steps:

(1) Define study region and crop of interest
(2) Download and preprocess NDVI and rainfall data
(3) Build a linear regression or random forest model
(4) Compare predictions with ground truth yield data

Expected Outcomes:

- Yield prediction map
- Model accuracy report
- 3–5 page summary report

Estimated Duration:

2–3 weeks

SDG Alignment:

SDG 2 – Zero Hunger, SDG 13 – Climate Action

Mini-Project 2: Geospatial AI in Forestry

Project Title:

Detecting Deforestation and Forest Fragmentation Using Deep Learning

Background & Motivation:

Deforestation is a key driver of climate change and biodiversity loss. This project applies
CNN-based classification to identify deforestation trends and fragmentation.

Objective:

Generate multi-temporal forest/non-forest maps and compute forest fragmentation index.

Tools & Technologies:

TensorFlow/Keras, Sentinel-2, QGIS, Google Earth Engine

Datasets Required:

- Sentinel-2 imagery
- Forest boundaries (Forest Survey of India)

Workflow Steps:

(1) Preprocess imagery for two time periods
(2) Train a CNN model for binary classification
(3) Apply the model to both time periods
(4) Use FRAGSTATS or QGIS plugins for fragmentation analysis

Expected Outcomes:

- Forest change maps
- Fragmentation metrics table
- Project report with analysis

Estimated Duration:

2–3 weeks

SDG Alignment:

SDG 15 – Life on Land, SDG 13 – Climate Action

Mini-Project 3: Geospatial AI in Water Resources

Project Title:

Monitoring Reservoir Storage Using SAR Imagery and Surface Water Detection

Background & Motivation:

Water stress affects agriculture and urban regions. Tracking seasonal surface water extent helps in planning resource allocation and assessing drought risk.

Objective:

Detect seasonal changes in reservoir water surface using Sentinel-1 SAR data.

Tools & Technologies:

Google Earth Engine, QGIS, SNAP toolbox

Datasets Required:

- Sentinel-1 SAR (GEE)
- Reservoir shapefiles (India WRIS)
- Rainfall data (IMD)

Workflow Steps:

(1) Select reservoir and time range

(2) Perform threshold-based water classification

(3) Plot surface area vs time

(4) Analyze correlation with rainfall and usage reports

Expected Outcomes:

- Time-series surface area change graph
- Maps showing seasonal extent
- Brief report with conclusions

Estimated Duration:

2–3 weeks

SDG Alignment:

SDG 6 – Clean Water, SDG 13 – Climate Action

Mini-Project 4: Deep Learning + Policy Frameworks & SDGs

Project Title:

Creating a Geospatial Dashboard for SDG 13 Using Open Datasets

Background & Motivation:

Geospatial visualizations aligned with the UN SDG indicators can help governments and NGOs track climate performance. This project builds a simple policy dashboard prototype.

Objective:

Integrate multiple geospatial layers into a dashboard to visualize climate stress zones.

Tools & Technologies:

Python (Dash/Streamlit), GEE, QGIS

Datasets Required:

- Forest loss (Global Forest Watch)
- Water bodies (India WRIS)
- Temperature trends (IMD)
- Urban growth (MODIS LULC)

Workflow Steps:

(1) Collect and process all geospatial layers
(2) Normalize and standardize datasets
(3) Create an interactive dashboard
(4) Link visualizations to specific SDG 13 targets

Expected Outcomes:

- Prototype dashboard

- 5–10 minute student presentation
- Policy summary connecting outputs to SDG indicators

Estimated Duration:

3–4 weeks

SDG Alignment:

SDG 13 – Climate Action, SDG 17 – Partnerships for the Goals

Bibliography

[1] I. Goodfellow, Y. Bengio, and A. Courville, *Deep Learning*. MIT Press, 2016. http://www.deeplearningbook.org.

[2] F. Chollet, *Deep Learning with Python*. Shelter Island, NY: Manning Publications, 1st ed., 2017.

[3] W. H. Maravilla, S. Basu, Q. Afreen, A. Basumatary, J. Manrique, P. Goswami, K. Milek, V. S., B. Roobin, J. Mushori, and J. Matu, *Leveraging AI for Sustainable Development: Diverse Applications Across SDG Goals*. 02 2025.

[4] M. Wegmann *et al.*, *Remote Sensing and GIS for Ecologists: Using Open Source Software*. Pelagic Publishing, 2016.

[5] A. Géron, *Hands-On Machine Learning with Scikit-Learn, Keras, and TensorFlow*. Beijing: O'Reilly Media, 2019.

[6] A. W. Kiwelekar, G. S. Mahamunkar, L. D. Netak, and V. B. Nikam, *Deep Learning Techniques for Geospatial Data Analysis*, pp. 63–81. Cham: Springer International Publishing, 2020.

[7] L. Zhang, L. Zhang, and B. Du, "Deep learning for remote sensing data: A technical tutorial on the state of the art," *IEEE Geoscience and remote sensing magazine*, vol. 4, no. 2, pp. 22–40, 2016.

[8] X. Zhu, D. Tuia, L. Mou, G.-S. Xia, L. Zhang, F. Xu, and F. Fraundorfer, "Deep learning in remote sensing: A review," *IEEE Geoscience and Remote Sensing Magazine (GRSM)*, 10 2017.

[9] L. U. Khan, I. Yaqoob, N. Tran, S. Kazmi, T. Nguyen Dang, and C. S. Hong, "Edge-computing-enabled smart cities: A comprehensive survey," *IEEE Internet of Things Journal*, vol. PP, pp. 1–1, 04 2020.

[10] G. Mai, Y. Xie, X. Jia, N. Lao, J. Rao, Q. Zhu, Z. Liu, Y.-Y. Chiang, and J. Jiao, "Towards the next generation of geospatial artificial intelligence," *International Journal of Applied Earth Observation and Geoinformation*, vol. 136, p. 104368, 2025.

[11] H. B. McMahan *et al.*, "Communication-efficient learning of deep networks from decentralized data," *AISTATS 2017*, pp. 1273–1282, 2017.

[12] G. S. Mahamunkar, "Dataset creation and comparative analysis of machine learning models for mangrove classification in coastal maharashtra, india," *International Journal on Recent and Innovation Trends in Computing and Communication*, vol. 12, no. 2, pp. 344–350, 2024.

[13] G. Mahamunkar, A. Kiwelekar, and L. Netak, "Deep learning model for black spot classification," *International Journal of Performability Engineering*, vol. 18, no. 3, p. 222, 2022.

[14] G. Mahamunkar, A. Kiwelekar, and L. Netak, "Landslide prediction using multi-layer perceptron model," in *Intelligent Computing* (K. Arai, ed.), (Cham), pp. 398–407, Springer Nature Switzerland, 2023.

[15] G. S. Mahamunkar and L. D. Netak, "Comparison of various deep cnn models for land use and land cover classification," in *Intelligent Human Computer Interaction* (J.-H. Kim, M. Singh, J. Khan, U. S. Tiwary, M. Sur, and D. Singh, eds.), (Cham), pp. 499–510, Springer International Publishing, 2022.

[16] G. S. Mahamunkar, A. W. Kiwelekar, and L. D. Netak, "Mapping and change detection of mangroves using remote sensing and google earth engine: A case study," in *ICT Systems and Sustainability* (M. Tuba, S. Akashe, and A. Joshi, eds.), (Singapore), pp. 187–195, Springer Nature Singapore, 2022.

[17] Google, "Google earth engine documentation." `https://developers.google.com/earth-engine`, 2021.

[18] Zenodo, "Zenodo: Open access repository." `https://zenodo.org`, 2021.

[19] GitHub, "Github repository for geospatial ai projects." `https://github.com`, 2021.